Country Music: A Very Short Introduction

VERY SHORT INTRODUCTIONS are for anyone wanting a stimulating and accessible way into a new subject. They are written by experts, and have been translated into more than 45 different languages.

The series began in 1995, and now covers a wide variety of topics in every discipline. The VSI library currently contains over 550 volumes—a Very Short Introduction to everything from Psychology and Philosophy of Science to American History and Relativity—and continues to grow in every subject area.

Very Short Introductions available now:

ABOLITIONISM Richard S. Newman
ACCOUNTING Christopher Nobes
ADAM SMITH Christopher J. Berry
ADOLESCENCE Peter K. Smith
ADVERTISING Winston Fletcher
AFRICAN AMERICAN RELIGION
    Eddie S. Glaude Jr.
AFRICAN HISTORY John Parker and
    Richard Rathbone
AFRICAN POLITICS Ian Taylor
AFRICAN RELIGIONS
    Jacob K. Olupona
AGEING Nancy A. Pachana
AGNOSTICISM Robin Le Poidevin
AGRICULTURE Paul Brassley and
    Richard Soffe
ALEXANDER THE GREAT
    Hugh Bowden
ALGEBRA Peter M. Higgins
AMERICAN CULTURAL HISTORY
    Eric Avila
AMERICAN FOREIGN RELATIONS
    Andrew Preston
AMERICAN HISTORY
    Paul S. Boyer
AMERICAN IMMIGRATION
    David A. Gerber
AMERICAN LEGAL HISTORY
    G. Edward White
AMERICAN NAVAL HISTORY
    Craig L. Symonds
AMERICAN POLITICAL HISTORY
    Donald Critchlow
AMERICAN POLITICAL PARTIES
    AND ELECTIONS L. Sandy Maisel

AMERICAN POLITICS
    Richard M. Valelly
THE AMERICAN PRESIDENCY
    Charles O. Jones
THE AMERICAN REVOLUTION
    Robert J. Allison
AMERICAN SLAVERY
    Heather Andrea Williams
THE AMERICAN WEST Stephen Aron
AMERICAN WOMEN'S HISTORY
    Susan Ware
ANAESTHESIA Aidan O'Donnell
ANALYTIC PHILOSOPHY
    Michael Beaney
ANARCHISM Colin Ward
ANCIENT ASSYRIA Karen Radner
ANCIENT EGYPT Ian Shaw
ANCIENT EGYPTIAN ART AND
    ARCHITECTURE Christina Riggs
ANCIENT GREECE Paul Cartledge
THE ANCIENT NEAR EAST
    Amanda H. Podany
ANCIENT PHILOSOPHY Julia Annas
ANCIENT WARFARE
    Harry Sidebottom
ANGELS David Albert Jones
ANGLICANISM Mark Chapman
THE ANGLO-SAXON AGE John Blair
ANIMAL BEHAVIOUR
    Tristram D. Wyatt
THE ANIMAL KINGDOM
    Peter Holland
ANIMAL RIGHTS David DeGrazia
THE ANTARCTIC Klaus Dodds
ANTHROPOCENE Erle C. Ellis

ANTISEMITISM Steven Beller
ANXIETY Daniel Freeman and
    Jason Freeman
APPLIED MATHEMATICS
    Alain Goriely
THE APOCRYPHAL GOSPELS
    Paul Foster
ARCHAEOLOGY Paul Bahn
ARCHITECTURE Andrew Ballantyne
ARISTOCRACY William Doyle
ARISTOTLE Jonathan Barnes
ART HISTORY Dana Arnold
ART THEORY Cynthia Freeland
ARTIFICIAL INTELLIGENCE
    Margaret A. Boden
ASIAN AMERICAN HISTORY
    Madeline Y. Hsu
ASTROBIOLOGY David C. Catling
ASTROPHYSICS James Binney
ATHEISM Julian Baggini
THE ATMOSPHERE Paul I. Palmer
AUGUSTINE Henry Chadwick
AUSTRALIA Kenneth Morgan
AUTISM Uta Frith
AUTOBIOGRAPHY Laura Marcus
THE AVANT GARDE David Cottington
THE AZTECS David Carrasco
BABYLONIA Trevor Bryce
BACTERIA Sebastian G. B. Amyes
BANKING John Goddard and
    John O. S. Wilson
BARTHES Jonathan Culler
THE BEATS David Sterritt
BEAUTY Roger Scruton
BEHAVIOURAL ECONOMICS
    Michelle Baddeley
BESTSELLERS John Sutherland
THE BIBLE John Riches
BIBLICAL ARCHAEOLOGY
    Eric H. Cline
BIG DATA Dawn E. Holmes
BIOGRAPHY Hermione Lee
BIOMETRICS Michael Fairhurst
BLACK HOLES Katherine Blundell
BLOOD Chris Cooper
THE BLUES Elijah Wald
THE BODY Chris Shilling
THE BOOK OF COMMON PRAYER
    Brian Cummings
THE BOOK OF MORMON
    Terryl Givens

BORDERS Alexander C. Diener and
    Joshua Hagen
THE BRAIN Michael O'Shea
BRANDING Robert Jones
THE BRICS Andrew F. Cooper
THE BRITISH CONSTITUTION
    Martin Loughlin
THE BRITISH EMPIRE
    Ashley Jackson
BRITISH POLITICS Anthony Wright
BUDDHA Michael Carrithers
BUDDHISM Damien Keown
BUDDHIST ETHICS Damien Keown
BYZANTIUM Peter Sarris
C. S. LEWIS James Como
CALVINISM Jon Balserak
CANCER Nicholas James
CAPITALISM James Fulcher
CATHOLICISM Gerald O'Collins
CAUSATION Stephen Mumford and
    Rani Lill Anjum
THE CELL Terence Allen and
    Graham Cowling
THE CELTS Barry Cunliffe
CHAOS Leonard Smith
CHARLES DICKENS Jenny Hartley
CHEMISTRY Peter Atkins
CHILD PSYCHOLOGY Usha Goswami
CHILDREN'S LITERATURE
    Kimberley Reynolds
CHINESE LITERATURE Sabina Knight
CHOICE THEORY Michael Allingham
CHRISTIAN ART Beth Williamson
CHRISTIAN ETHICS D. Stephen Long
CHRISTIANITY Linda Woodhead
CIRCADIAN RHYTHMS
    Russell Foster and Leon Kreitzman
CITIZENSHIP Richard Bellamy
CIVIL ENGINEERING
    David Muir Wood
CLASSICAL LITERATURE William Allan
CLASSICAL MYTHOLOGY
    Helen Morales
CLASSICS Mary Beard and
    John Henderson
CLAUSEWITZ Michael Howard
CLIMATE Mark Maslin
CLIMATE CHANGE Mark Maslin
CLINICAL PSYCHOLOGY
    Susan Llewelyn and
    Katie Aafjes-van Doorn

COGNITIVE NEUROSCIENCE
    Richard Passingham
THE COLD WAR Robert McMahon
COLONIAL AMERICA Alan Taylor
COLONIAL LATIN AMERICAN
    LITERATURE Rolena Adorno
COMBINATORICS Robin Wilson
COMEDY Matthew Bevis
COMMUNISM Leslie Holmes
COMPARATIVE LITERATURE
    Ben Hutchinson
COMPLEXITY John H. Holland
THE COMPUTER Darrel Ince
COMPUTER SCIENCE
    Subrata Dasgupta
CONCENTRATION CAMPS Dan Stone
CONFUCIANISM Daniel K. Gardner
THE CONQUISTADORS
    Matthew Restall and
    Felipe Fernández-Armesto
CONSCIENCE Paul Strohm
CONSCIOUSNESS Susan Blackmore
CONTEMPORARY ART
    Julian Stallabrass
CONTEMPORARY FICTION
    Robert Eaglestone
CONTINENTAL PHILOSOPHY
    Simon Critchley
COPERNICUS Owen Gingerich
CORAL REEFS Charles Sheppard
CORPORATE SOCIAL
    RESPONSIBILITY
    Jeremy Moon
CORRUPTION Leslie Holmes
COSMOLOGY Peter Coles
CRIME FICTION Richard Bradford
CRIMINAL JUSTICE Julian V. Roberts
CRIMINOLOGY Tim Newburn
CRITICAL THEORY
    Stephen Eric Bronner
THE CRUSADES Christopher Tyerman
CRYPTOGRAPHY Fred Piper and
    Sean Murphy
CRYSTALLOGRAPHY A. M. Glazer
THE CULTURAL REVOLUTION
    Richard Curt Kraus
DADA AND SURREALISM
    David Hopkins
DANTE Peter Hainsworth and
    David Robey
DARWIN Jonathan Howard

THE DEAD SEA SCROLLS
    Timothy H. Lim
DECADENCE David Weir
DECOLONIZATION Dane Kennedy
DEMOCRACY Bernard Crick
DEMOGRAPHY Sarah Harper
DEPRESSION Jan Scott and
    Mary Jane Tacchi
DERRIDA Simon Glendinning
DESCARTES Tom Sorell
DESERTS Nick Middleton
DESIGN John Heskett
DEVELOPMENT Ian Goldin
DEVELOPMENTAL BIOLOGY
    Lewis Wolpert
THE DEVIL Darren Oldridge
DIASPORA Kevin Kenny
DICTIONARIES Lynda Mugglestone
DINOSAURS David Norman
DIPLOMACY Joseph M. Siracusa
DOCUMENTARY FILM
    Patricia Aufderheide
DREAMING J. Allan Hobson
DRUGS Les Iversen
DRUIDS Barry Cunliffe
DYSLEXIA Margaret J. Snowling
EARLY MUSIC Thomas Forrest Kelly
THE EARTH Martin Redfern
EARTH SYSTEM SCIENCE Tim Lenton
ECONOMICS Partha Dasgupta
EDUCATION Gary Thomas
EGYPTIAN MYTH Geraldine Pinch
EIGHTEENTH-CENTURY BRITAIN
    Paul Langford
THE ELEMENTS Philip Ball
EMOTION Dylan Evans
EMPIRE Stephen Howe
ENGELS Terrell Carver
ENGINEERING David Blockley
THE ENGLISH LANGUAGE
    Simon Horobin
ENGLISH LITERATURE
    Jonathan Bate
THE ENLIGHTENMENT
    John Robertson
ENTREPRENEURSHIP
    Paul Westhead and Mike Wright
ENVIRONMENTAL ECONOMICS
    Stephen Smith
ENVIRONMENTAL ETHICS
    Robin Attfield

ENVIRONMENTAL LAW
    Elizabeth Fisher
ENVIRONMENTAL POLITICS
    Andrew Dobson
EPICUREANISM Catherine Wilson
EPIDEMIOLOGY Rodolfo Saracci
ETHICS Simon Blackburn
ETHNOMUSICOLOGY Timothy Rice
THE ETRUSCANS Christopher Smith
EUGENICS Philippa Levine
THE EUROPEAN UNION
    Simon Usherwood and John Pinder
EUROPEAN UNION LAW
    Anthony Arnull
EVOLUTION Brian and
    Deborah Charlesworth
EXISTENTIALISM Thomas Flynn
EXPLORATION Stewart A. Weaver
EXTINCTION Paul B. Wignall
THE EYE Michael Land
FAIRY TALE Marina Warner
FAMILY LAW Jonathan Herring
FASCISM Kevin Passmore
FASHION Rebecca Arnold
FEMINISM Margaret Walters
FILM Michael Wood
FILM MUSIC Kathryn Kalinak
FILM NOIR James Naremore
THE FIRST WORLD WAR
    Michael Howard
FOLK MUSIC Mark Slobin
FOOD John Krebs
FORENSIC PSYCHOLOGY David Canter
FORENSIC SCIENCE Jim Fraser
FORESTS Jaboury Ghazoul
FOSSILS Keith Thomson
FOUCAULT Gary Gutting
THE FOUNDING FATHERS
    R. B. Bernstein
FRACTALS Kenneth Falconer
FREE SPEECH Nigel Warburton
FREE WILL Thomas Pink
FREEMASONRY Andreas Önnerfors
FRENCH LITERATURE John D. Lyons
THE FRENCH REVOLUTION
    William Doyle
FREUD Anthony Storr
FUNDAMENTALISM Malise Ruthven
FUNGI Nicholas P. Money
THE FUTURE Jennifer M. Gidley
GALAXIES John Gribbin

GALILEO Stillman Drake
GAME THEORY Ken Binmore
GANDHI Bhikhu Parekh
GARDEN HISTORY Gordon Campbell
GEOFFREY CHAUCER David Wallace
GENES Jonathan Slack
GENIUS Andrew Robinson
GENOMICS John Archibald
GEOGRAPHY John Matthews and
    David Herbert
GEOLOGY Jan Zalasiewicz
GEOPHYSICS William Lowrie
GEOPOLITICS Klaus Dodds
GERMAN LITERATURE Nicholas Boyle
GERMAN PHILOSOPHY
    Andrew Bowie
GLACIATION David J. A. Evans
GLOBAL CATASTROPHES Bill McGuire
GLOBAL ECONOMIC HISTORY
    Robert C. Allen
GLOBALIZATION Manfred Steger
GOD John Bowker
GOETHE Ritchie Robertson
THE GOTHIC Nick Groom
GOVERNANCE Mark Bevir
GRAVITY Timothy Clifton
THE GREAT DEPRESSION AND THE
    NEW DEAL
    Eric Rauchway
HABERMAS James Gordon Finlayson
THE HABSBURG EMPIRE
    Martyn Rady
HAPPINESS Daniel M. Haybron
THE HARLEM RENAISSANCE
    Cheryl A. Wall
THE HEBREW BIBLE AS LITERATURE
    Tod Linafelt
HEGEL Peter Singer
HEIDEGGER Michael Inwood
THE HELLENISTIC AGE
    Peter Thonemann
HEREDITY John Waller
HERMENEUTICS Jens Zimmermann
HERODOTUS Jennifer T. Roberts
HIEROGLYPHS Penelope Wilson
HINDUISM Kim Knott
HISTORY John H. Arnold
THE HISTORY OF ASTRONOMY
    Michael Hoskin
THE HISTORY OF CHEMISTRY
    William H. Brock

THE HISTORY OF CHILDHOOD
  James Marten
THE HISTORY OF CINEMA
  Geoffrey Nowell-Smith
THE HISTORY OF LIFE
  Michael Benton
THE HISTORY OF MATHEMATICS
  Jacqueline Stedall
THE HISTORY OF MEDICINE
  William Bynum
THE HISTORY OF PHYSICS
  J. L. Heilbron
THE HISTORY OF TIME
  Leofranc Holford-Strevens
HIV AND AIDS Alan Whiteside
HOBBES Richard Tuck
HOLLYWOOD Peter Decherney
THE HOLY ROMAN EMPIRE
  Joachim Whaley
HOME Michael Allen Fox
HOMER Barbara Graziosi
HORMONES Martin Luck
HUMAN ANATOMY Leslie Klenerman
HUMAN EVOLUTION Bernard Wood
HUMAN RIGHTS Andrew Clapham
HUMANISM Stephen Law
HUME A. J. Ayer
HUMOUR Noël Carroll
THE ICE AGE Jamie Woodward
IDENTITY Florian Coulmas
IDEOLOGY Michael Freeden
THE IMMUNE SYSTEM
  Paul Klenerman
INDIAN CINEMA Ashish
  Rajadhyaksha
INDIAN PHILOSOPHY Sue Hamilton
THE INDUSTRIAL REVOLUTION
  Robert C. Allen
INFECTIOUS DISEASE Marta L. Wayne
  and Benjamin M. Bolker
INFINITY Ian Stewart
INFORMATION Luciano Floridi
INNOVATION Mark Dodgson and
  David Gann
INTELLECTUAL PROPERTY
  Siva Vaidhyanathan
INTELLIGENCE Ian J. Deary
INTERNATIONAL LAW
  Vaughan Lowe
INTERNATIONAL MIGRATION
  Khalid Koser

INTERNATIONAL RELATIONS
  Paul Wilkinson
INTERNATIONAL SECURITY
  Christopher S. Browning
IRAN Ali M. Ansari
ISLAM Malise Ruthven
ISLAMIC HISTORY Adam Silverstein
ISOTOPES Rob Ellam
ITALIAN LITERATURE
  Peter Hainsworth and David Robey
JESUS Richard Bauckham
JEWISH HISTORY David N. Myers
JOURNALISM Ian Hargreaves
JUDAISM Norman Solomon
JUNG Anthony Stevens
KABBALAH Joseph Dan
KAFKA Ritchie Robertson
KANT Roger Scruton
KEYNES Robert Skidelsky
KIERKEGAARD Patrick Gardiner
KNOWLEDGE Jennifer Nagel
THE KORAN Michael Cook
LAKES Warwick F. Vincent
LANDSCAPE ARCHITECTURE
  Ian H. Thompson
LANDSCAPES AND
  GEOMORPHOLOGY
  Andrew Goudie and Heather Viles
LANGUAGES Stephen R. Anderson
LATE ANTIQUITY Gillian Clark
LAW Raymond Wacks
THE LAWS OF THERMODYNAMICS
  Peter Atkins
LEADERSHIP Keith Grint
LEARNING Mark Haselgrove
LEIBNIZ Maria Rosa Antognazza
LIBERALISM Michael Freeden
LIGHT Ian Walmsley
LINCOLN Allen C. Guelzo
LINGUISTICS Peter Matthews
LITERARY THEORY Jonathan Culler
LOCKE John Dunn
LOGIC Graham Priest
LOVE Ronald de Sousa
MACHIAVELLI Quentin Skinner
MADNESS Andrew Scull
MAGIC Owen Davies
MAGNA CARTA Nicholas Vincent
MAGNETISM Stephen Blundell
MALTHUS Donald Winch
MAMMALS T. S. Kemp

MANAGEMENT John Hendry
MAO Delia Davin
MARINE BIOLOGY Philip V. Mladenov
THE MARQUIS DE SADE John Phillips
MARTIN LUTHER Scott H. Hendrix
MARTYRDOM Jolyon Mitchell
MARX Peter Singer
MATERIALS Christopher Hall
MATHEMATICAL FINANCE
    Mark H. A. Davis
MATHEMATICS Timothy Gowers
MATTER Geoff Cottrell
THE MEANING OF LIFE
    Terry Eagleton
MEASUREMENT David Hand
MEDICAL ETHICS Michael Dunn and
    Tony Hope
MEDICAL LAW Charles Foster
MEDIEVAL BRITAIN John Gillingham
    and Ralph A. Griffiths
MEDIEVAL LITERATURE
    Elaine Treharne
MEDIEVAL PHILOSOPHY
    John Marenbon
MEMORY Jonathan K. Foster
METAPHYSICS Stephen Mumford
METHODISM William J. Abraham
THE MEXICAN REVOLUTION
    Alan Knight
MICHAEL FARADAY
    Frank A. J. L. James
MICROBIOLOGY Nicholas P. Money
MICROECONOMICS Avinash Dixit
MICROSCOPY Terence Allen
THE MIDDLE AGES Miri Rubin
MILITARY JUSTICE Eugene R. Fidell
MILITARY STRATEGY
    Antulio J. Echevarria II
MINERALS David Vaughan
MIRACLES Yujin Nagasawa
MODERN ARCHITECTURE
    Adam Sharr
MODERN ART David Cottington
MODERN CHINA Rana Mitter
MODERN DRAMA
    Kirsten E. Shepherd-Barr
MODERN FRANCE
    Vanessa R. Schwartz
MODERN INDIA Craig Jeffrey
MODERN IRELAND Senia Pašeta
MODERN ITALY Anna Cento Bull

MODERN JAPAN
    Christopher Goto-Jones
MODERN LATIN AMERICAN
    LITERATURE
    Roberto González Echevarría
MODERN WAR Richard English
MODERNISM Christopher Butler
MOLECULAR BIOLOGY
    Aysha Divan and Janice A. Royds
MOLECULES Philip Ball
MONASTICISM Stephen J. Davis
THE MONGOLS Morris Rossabi
MOONS David A. Rothery
MORMONISM
    Richard Lyman Bushman
MOUNTAINS Martin F. Price
MUHAMMAD Jonathan A. C. Brown
MULTICULTURALISM Ali Rattansi
MULTILINGUALISM John C. Maher
MUSIC Nicholas Cook
MYTH Robert A. Segal
NAPOLEON David Bell
THE NAPOLEONIC WARS
    Mike Rapport
NATIONALISM Steven Grosby
NATIVE AMERICAN LITERATURE
    Sean Teuton
NAVIGATION Jim Bennett
NAZI GERMANY Jane Caplan
NELSON MANDELA Elleke Boehmer
NEOLIBERALISM Manfred Steger and
    Ravi Roy
NETWORKS Guido Caldarelli and
    Michele Catanzaro
THE NEW TESTAMENT
    Luke Timothy Johnson
THE NEW TESTAMENT AS
    LITERATURE Kyle Keefer
NEWTON Robert Iliffe
NIETZSCHE Michael Tanner
NINETEENTH-CENTURY BRITAIN
    Christopher Harvie and
    H. C. G. Matthew
THE NORMAN CONQUEST
    George Garnett
NORTH AMERICAN INDIANS
    Theda Perdue and
    Michael D. Green
NORTHERN IRELAND
    Marc Mulholland
NOTHING Frank Close

NUCLEAR PHYSICS Frank Close
NUCLEAR POWER Maxwell Irvine
NUCLEAR WEAPONS
    Joseph M. Siracusa
NUMBERS Peter M. Higgins
NUTRITION David A. Bender
OBJECTIVITY Stephen Gaukroger
OCEANS Dorrik Stow
THE OLD TESTAMENT
    Michael D. Coogan
THE ORCHESTRA D. Kern Holoman
ORGANIC CHEMISTRY
    Graham Patrick
ORGANIZATIONS Mary Jo Hatch
ORGANIZED CRIME
    Georgios A. Antonopoulos and
    Georgios Papanicolaou
ORTHODOX CHRISTIANITY
    A. Edward Siecienski
PAGANISM Owen Davies
PAIN Rob Boddice
THE PALESTINIAN-ISRAELI
    CONFLICT Martin Bunton
PANDEMICS Christian W. McMillen
PARTICLE PHYSICS Frank Close
PAUL E. P. Sanders
PEACE Oliver P. Richmond
PENTECOSTALISM William K. Kay
PERCEPTION Brian Rogers
THE PERIODIC TABLE Eric R. Scerri
PHILOSOPHY Edward Craig
PHILOSOPHY IN THE ISLAMIC
    WORLD Peter Adamson
PHILOSOPHY OF LAW
    Raymond Wacks
PHILOSOPHY OF SCIENCE
    Samir Okasha
PHILOSOPHY OF RELIGION
    Tim Bayne
PHOTOGRAPHY Steve Edwards
PHYSICAL CHEMISTRY Peter Atkins
PHYSICS Sidney Perkowitz
PILGRIMAGE Ian Reader
PLAGUE Paul Slack
PLANETS David A. Rothery
PLANTS Timothy Walker
PLATE TECTONICS Peter Molnar
PLATO Julia Annas
POLITICAL PHILOSOPHY
    David Miller
POLITICS Kenneth Minogue
POPULISM Cas Mudde and
    Cristóbal Rovira Kaltwasser
POSTCOLONIALISM Robert Young
POSTMODERNISM Christopher Butler
POSTSTRUCTURALISM
    Catherine Belsey
POVERTY Philip N. Jefferson
PREHISTORY Chris Gosden
PRESOCRATIC PHILOSOPHY
    Catherine Osborne
PRIVACY Raymond Wacks
PROBABILITY John Haigh
PROGRESSIVISM Walter Nugent
PROJECTS Andrew Davies
PROTESTANTISM Mark A. Noll
PSYCHIATRY Tom Burns
PSYCHOANALYSIS Daniel Pick
PSYCHOLOGY Gillian Butler and
    Freda McManus
PSYCHOLOGY OF MUSIC
    Elizabeth Hellmuth Margulis
PSYCHOTHERAPY Tom Burns and
    Eva Burns-Lundgren
PUBLIC ADMINISTRATION
    Stella Z. Theodoulou and Ravi K. Roy
PUBLIC HEALTH Virginia Berridge
PURITANISM Francis J. Bremer
THE QUAKERS Pink Dandelion
QUANTUM THEORY
    John Polkinghorne
RACISM Ali Rattansi
RADIOACTIVITY Claudio Tuniz
RASTAFARI Ennis B. Edmonds
READING Belinda Jack
THE REAGAN REVOLUTION Gil Troy
REALITY Jan Westerhoff
THE REFORMATION Peter Marshall
RELATIVITY Russell Stannard
RELIGION IN AMERICA Timothy Beal
THE RENAISSANCE Jerry Brotton
RENAISSANCE ART
    Geraldine A. Johnson
REPTILES T. S. Kemp
REVOLUTIONS Jack A. Goldstone
RHETORIC Richard Toye
RISK Baruch Fischhoff and John Kadvany
RITUAL Barry Stephenson
RIVERS Nick Middleton
ROBOTICS Alan Winfield
ROCKS Jan Zalasiewicz
ROMAN BRITAIN Peter Salway

THE ROMAN EMPIRE
    Christopher Kelly
THE ROMAN REPUBLIC
    David M. Gwynn
ROMANTICISM Michael Ferber
ROUSSEAU Robert Wokler
RUSSELL A. C. Grayling
RUSSIAN HISTORY Geoffrey Hosking
RUSSIAN LITERATURE Catriona Kelly
THE RUSSIAN REVOLUTION
    S. A. Smith
THE SAINTS Simon Yarrow
SAVANNAS Peter A. Furley
SCHIZOPHRENIA Chris Frith and
    Eve Johnstone
SCHOPENHAUER
    Christopher Janaway
SCIENCE AND RELIGION
    Thomas Dixon
SCIENCE FICTION David Seed
THE SCIENTIFIC REVOLUTION
    Lawrence M. Principe
SCOTLAND Rab Houston
SECULARISM Andrew Copson
SEXUAL SELECTION Marlene Zuk and
    Leigh W. Simmons
SEXUALITY Véronique Mottier
SHAKESPEARE'S COMEDIES
    Bart van Es
SHAKESPEARE'S SONNETS AND
    POEMS Jonathan F. S. Post
SHAKESPEARE'S TRAGEDIES
    Stanley Wells
SIKHISM Eleanor Nesbitt
THE SILK ROAD James A. Millward
SLANG Jonathon Green
SLEEP Steven W. Lockley and
    Russell G. Foster
SOCIAL AND CULTURAL
    ANTHROPOLOGY
    John Monaghan and Peter Just
SOCIAL PSYCHOLOGY Richard J. Crisp
SOCIAL WORK Sally Holland and
    Jonathan Scourfield
SOCIALISM Michael Newman
SOCIOLINGUISTICS John Edwards
SOCIOLOGY Steve Bruce
SOCRATES C. C. W. Taylor
SOUND Mike Goldsmith
SOUTHEAST ASIA James R. Rush
THE SOVIET UNION Stephen Lovell

THE SPANISH CIVIL WAR
    Helen Graham
SPANISH LITERATURE Jo Labanyi
SPINOZA Roger Scruton
SPIRITUALITY Philip Sheldrake
SPORT Mike Cronin
STARS Andrew King
STATISTICS David J. Hand
STEM CELLS Jonathan Slack
STOICISM Brad Inwood
STRUCTURAL ENGINEERING
    David Blockley
STUART BRITAIN John Morrill
SUPERCONDUCTIVITY
    Stephen Blundell
SYMMETRY Ian Stewart
SYNAESTHESIA Julia Simner
SYNTHETIC BIOLOGY Jamie A. Davies
TAXATION Stephen Smith
TEETH Peter S. Ungar
TELESCOPES Geoff Cottrell
TERRORISM Charles Townshend
THEATRE Marvin Carlson
THEOLOGY David F. Ford
THINKING AND REASONING
    Jonathan St B. T. Evans
THOMAS AQUINAS Fergus Kerr
THOUGHT Tim Bayne
TIBETAN BUDDHISM
    Matthew T. Kapstein
TOCQUEVILLE Harvey C. Mansfield
TOLSTOY Liza Knapp
TRAGEDY Adrian Poole
TRANSLATION Matthew Reynolds
THE TREATY OF VERSAILLES
    Michael S. Neiberg
THE TROJAN WAR Eric H. Cline
TRUST Katherine Hawley
THE TUDORS John Guy
TWENTIETH-CENTURY BRITAIN
    Kenneth O. Morgan
TYPOGRAPHY Paul Luna
THE UNITED NATIONS
    Jussi M. Hanhimäki
UNIVERSITIES AND COLLEGES
    David Palfreyman and
    Paul Temple
THE U.S. CONGRESS
    Donald A. Ritchie
THE U.S. CONSTITUTION
    David J. Bodenhamer

THE U.S. SUPREME COURT
    Linda Greenhouse
UTILITARIANISM
    Katarzyna de Lazari-Radek and
    Peter Singer
UTOPIANISM Lyman Tower Sargent
VETERINARY SCIENCE James Yeates
THE VIKINGS Julian D. Richards
VIRUSES Dorothy H. Crawford
VOLTAIRE Nicholas Cronk
WAR AND TECHNOLOGY
    Alex Roland
WATER John Finney
WAVES Mike Goldsmith

WEATHER Storm Dunlop
THE WELFARE STATE David Garland
WILLIAM SHAKESPEARE Stanley Wells
WITCHCRAFT Malcolm Gaskill
WITTGENSTEIN A. C. Grayling
WORK Stephen Fineman
WORLD MUSIC Philip Bohlman
THE WORLD TRADE
    ORGANIZATION
    Amrita Narlikar
WORLD WAR II Gerhard L. Weinberg
WRITING AND SCRIPT
    Andrew Robinson
ZIONISM Michael Stanislawski

Available soon:

PSYCHOPATHY Essi Viding
POETRY Bernard O'Donoghue
ENERGY SYSTEMS Nick Jenkins

ALBERT CAMUS
    Oliver Gloag
DYNASTY Jeroen Duindam

For more information visit our website

www.oup.com/vsi/

Richard Carlin

COUNTRY MUSIC

A Very Short Introduction

OXFORD
UNIVERSITY PRESS

OXFORD
UNIVERSITY PRESS

Oxford University Press is a department of the University of Oxford.
It furthers the University's objective of excellence in research, scholarship,
and education by publishing worldwide. Oxford is a registered trade mark of
Oxford University Press in the UK and certain other countries.

Published in the United States of America by Oxford University Press
198 Madison Avenue, New York, NY 10016, United States of America.

Oxford University Press 2019

All rights reserved. No part of this publication may be reproduced,
stored in a retrieval system, or transmitted, in any form or by any means,
without the prior permission in writing of Oxford University Press,
or as expressly permitted by law, by license, or under terms agreed with
the appropriate reproduction rights organization. Inquiries concerning
reproduction outside the scope of the above should be sent to the
Rights Department, Oxford University Press, at the address above.

You must not circulate this work in any other form
and you must impose this same condition on any acquirer.

Library of Congress Control Number: 2019945453

ISBN 9780190902841

1 3 5 7 9 8 6 4 2

Printed in Great Britain by
Ashford Colour Press Ltd., Gosport, Hants.

Contents

List of illustrations xv

Acknowledgments xvii

Introduction 1

1 Behind the "big bang": The roots of country music 4

2 "Wildwood flowers": Country music goes
   mainstream, 1923–1930 20

3 "Back in the saddle again": The birth of the singing
   cowboy, 1930–1945 35

4 "Honky-tonkin'": Postwar country music, 1945–1959 50

5 "Make the world go away": Countrypolitan sounds,
   1957–1964 65

6 "Mama tried": Country alternatives, 1965–1980 81

7 "Friends in low places": Retro-country and
   country-pop since 1980 97

   Coda: Country music in a new millennium 117

   Further reading 121

   Index 125

List of illustrations

1. Amateur banjo and guitar players **17**
   Author's collection

2. Ryman Auditorium, first home of the Grand Ole Opry **27**
   Library of Congress HABS TN-23

3. Carter family songbook, 1927 **32**
   Author's collection

4. Sheet music for "Blue Yodel No. 5" **34**
   Author's collection

5. Patsy Montana sheet music **39**
   Author's collection

6. The Blue Sky Boys, ca. 1935 **43**
   Author's collection

7. Hank and Audrey Williams and the Drifting Cowboys **55**
   Author's collection

8. Ferlin Huskey and Patsy Cline **69**
   Author's collection

9. Johnny Cash and June Carter Cash **91**
   Photo copyright/by permission of Perry Werner

10. John Hartford **93**
    Author's collection

11. The Judds **108**
    Author's collection

Acknowledgments

For advice in the past, present, and likely future, I wish to alphabetically thank: Moses Asch; Ben Bierman; Ken Bloom; Bob Carlin; Dale Cockrell; Ronald Cohen; Colin Escott; David Gahr; Mike Holmes; Richard Kassel; Rod Knight; Richard Kostelanetz; Kip Lornell; Michael Lydon; Chris and Angela Marianni-Smith; Dave Marsh; Fred W. and Gloria McDarrah; Jessica Myers; Jocelyn Neal; Jeff Place; Art Rosenbaum; Raeanne Rubinstein; Larry Sandberg; Henry Sapoznik; Atesh Sonneborn; Dick Weissman; Amy Whitmer; Charles Wolfe; and Alban Zak. This book is dedicated to the memory of Perry Werner.

Introduction

Cowboy hats, pickup trucks, tank tops, leather boots—country music has been defined as much by its symbols as it has by its sound. It is a music of timeless themes, telling stories of love gone wrong and families torn asunder; it's peopled by hard-drinkin', hard-fightin', and hard-workin' folks. It has both benefited from its association with the "old, strange America"—the so-called backwoods that are inhabited by the "unrefined" sons and daughters of the rough-hewn immigrants who first captured the land from its original owners—and been derided for this same association.

Branded as the music of hillbillies, hicks, and hayseeds, of rednecks and racists, country music is the poor stepchild of American popular musical styles, lacking the intellectual or street cred of jazz and blues, show tunes and soul, rock 'n' roll and rap. Yet, when more accurate ways of measuring record sales came into being, it became rapidly clear that country music is the most "popular" of all musical styles in terms of sheer numbers. And the music has stubbornly endured, just as its best performers never seem to retire. While occasionally it surfaces to the top of America's consciousness, it is country's deep-rooted, almost subterranean nature that has made it in many ways America's most profound indigenous pop music.

Inherently nostalgic, country music is accused of only looking backward, in its lyrics, politics, and musical style. But this is somewhat misleading, because, as with most dynamic, popular styles, there are always forces pushing forward, too, as new creative voices emerge. And, as in other musical styles, these new voices are often resisted by the old guard, who think they alone can legitimately define what constitutes "real" country music. This creative tension is behind the evolution of many subgenres, from the sentimental songs and old-time dance music of the '20s through the Western swing of the '30s and '40s and the honky-tonk of the later '40s and early '50s, to countrypolitan from the mid-'50s through the mid-'60s and country-pop in the '70s, through neotraditional and country-rock in the '80s and '90s, to bro country in the 2000s and 2010s, and so on and so on, every style having one foot in the past and one stepping toward the future. And like all popular music styles, the creative is constantly counterbalanced by the commercial—or at least the need to achieve a level of commercial success that can sustain a musical career. The gatekeepers try hard to define and contain a musical style that is, by its very nature, ever-changing and insistent on defining itself.

Although country values are often positioned against those of the city, country music's popularity is not limited to the so-called flyover states. Perhaps due to its association with rural life, country music has always fascinated city dwellers, who sentimentalize it as reflecting a simpler, easier way of American life. Nowadays, city dwellers may be embarrassed to say they love "country music," although they're quick to embrace so-called new genres like Americana, alt-folk, or retro-country—all of which are just country music dressed up in more appealing clothing. The Zen-like notion behind Kris Kristofferson's famous lyric "Freedom's just another word for nothing left to lose" is just another side of the more chest-thumping nationalistic ideals of freedom expressed in Lee Greenwood's "God Bless the U.S.A." Country songs have a way of sidestepping ideologies by being open to each listener's own interpretation, connecting rural and city ideals in unexpected ways.

Think of country music as a river: flowing along from a starting point in the distinctly American marriage of European and African American musical cultures; meandering through different regions; straying off the path from time to time; but always somehow regaining its footing. So this little book is not meant to "define" country music, but rather to dip its toes into the water from time to time, looking for commonalities and differences, expanding a bit to cover favorite styles and performers, and trying to be a trustworthy guide. You may disagree with the route that it follows or object to the selected stops along the way—so feel free to stray off the path and explore on your own. The music is wide ranging enough to encompass many different viewpoints.

Like all popular music styles, the best country music balances the personal with the commercial; it is both nostalgic and progressive, reflecting earlier influences while rejecting their limitations; and ultimately it is expressive of our cultural values—both the laudable and the lamented. This short book tracks it all—hopefully in a way that is both readable and provocative.

1

Behind the "big bang": The roots of country music

In late July of 1927, New York record producer and music publisher Ralph Peer showed up in a tiny Tennessee town on the Virginia border, carrying with him all the necessary equipment to set up a portable studio. He came to record then-bestselling country star Ernest Stoneman and his family, whom Peer had previously recorded for OKeh Records. Now working for Victor, Peer asked Stoneman how he could locate other acts that might have the same sales appeal as Stoneman's group. Stoneman told the producer that if he wanted to record "authentic" country, blues, and gospel music, he had to travel to where the music was made and not wait for groups to find their way to New York. Stoneman suggested that the producer make his base in Bristol, because it was the hub of the Tri-Cities region, then the largest urban area in the South. Lacking a proper recording studio, Peer found an open space above a hat factory, which was conveniently located right on the town's main street.

In anticipation of his trip, Peer had run newspaper ads announcing that he'd pay any artist $50 per accepted "side" (song recorded and issued) plus a small two-and-a-half-cent royalty on any sales. Not surprisingly, the first act Peer recorded was Stoneman and his group. Few others took up the offer until a local newspaper ran an article noting that Stoneman had made $3,600 in royalties on a single hit record—his recording of the old play-party song, "Skip to My Lou"—released in 1926. This article caught the eye of the mother of a member of a band called the Teneva Ramblers; the group originally hailed from Bristol and had been working on the radio out of Asheville, North Carolina. She urged them to return to Bristol, where they successfully auditioned for Peer. However, before actually recording, the band had a falling-out with their lead singer over how they would be credited on the record, so he ended up recording as a solo artist. That singer was Jimmie Rodgers, who recorded a single 78, "The Soldier's Sweetheart" backed with "Sleep, Baby, Sleep," thus earning the promised $100 for his work. The resulting 78 sold well enough to convince Peer to bring Rodgers to Victor's main studios in Camden, New Jersey, where he cut four more songs, including his signature, bestselling hit "Blue Yodel" (also known as "T for Texas"), launching his career.

Three days before Rodgers arrived in Bristol, another group made the journey to the town from their home base in rural southwest Virginia. Alvin Pleasant Carter (known as "A. P.") was a traveling fruit-tree salesman who was married to Sara Addington, a talented singer and autoharp player. Carter, Sara, and A. P.'s sister-in-law, Maybelle, would often sing together at home, particularly enjoying the popular sentimental songs of the day. Sara's deep lead voice was complemented by A. P.'s bass and Maybelle's tenor harmony; Maybelle had also developed a unique way of playing the guitar, connecting the individual chords by playing short runs on the bass strings. Peer had heard of the family and had written to them to let them know he'd be in Bristol, but he received no response. So when they showed up at his studio in late July, he was somewhat surprised to see them. His initial impression was not too positive. "They wander[ed] in," Peer told an interviewer in 1959. "He's dressed in overalls and the women are country women from way back there. They looked like hillbillies. But as soon as I heard Sara's voice, that was it. I knew it was going to be wonderful." On August 1, the group recorded four songs, two of which were issued by Victor the following November. Thus began the phenomenal career of the Carter Family.

Many scholars have come to view Peer's sessions in Bristol as a key date in country music history, dubbing it the "big bang" that ignited an entire industry. Like all founding myths, this somewhat simplifies the story: As early as 1922, there had been successful country recordings. But the presence in one place of these two seminal acts—representing as they did two important strands in the country style—was indeed an important event. It is possible to argue that Rodgers's blues-influenced singing represented one strand of the country sound, drawing on traditional African American music, while the Carters represented the other, the Anglo-American traditions. This of course is also an oversimplification, but it serves as a stepping-off point for our story. How did country music evolve? What were its antecedents? How did this unique style draw on different cultures to become a uniquely American creation?

"Old familiar tunes": Country music and its roots: Eighteenth century to 1920

Like most American musical forms, country music developed out of many different influences. Although viewed today as the music of white Southerners, it in fact includes strong elements of African American traditions, as we will see. Other groups—including Spanish, French, and Native American musicians—also added to the mix, as musical influences have always freely traveled from place to place. This chapter will explore those roots and how this music was initially documented and received by scholars, folklorists, and performers and songwriters themselves. It will also explore how selective aspects of these musical influences were used to market this music, particularly through new performance styles and music publishing.

Anglo-American traditions: Ballads, dance, and religious music

The music of the British Isles is remarkably diverse, with several types of music performed in a variety of styles and on different instruments. We will focus particularly on the sung tradition of folk balladry, music for dancing, and religious music for worship.

Ballads are long, narrative folk songs that often tell stories based on legend and myth. They are generally strophic (that is, they have a melodic structure that follows the lyrics and repeats as each new stanza is sung). They are usually sung by solo vocalists, in a "heightened" style that emphasized the fact that these songs were set apart from everyday experience. This could include heavy vocal ornamentation, use of falsetto, a tight-throated (nasal) vocal style, and other techniques that—like those of the best opera singers—were as much a part of the expressive culture of these songs as the melodies and texts themselves. Some of the greatest ballad singers in the American traditions—such as Dillard Chandler or Almeda Riddle—would apply their vocal techniques to all types of songs, elevating even popular numbers like the sentimental country hit "Old Shep" into the realm of high art.

The original scholars who collected ballads were primarily interested in the literary qualities of their lyrics. Some hoped to discover English-language sagas that would rival the ancient Greek epics. For this reason, most of these collectors published only the lyrics of these songs and ignored the singing traditions. Some drew from printed sources rather than singers themselves. The best-known American collector was the Harvard English professor Francis James Child, whose five-volume collection of ballads—compiled over the last two decades of the nineteenth century—established certain songs as being "true" ballads. Child created a numbering system that is still in use today; more recent or topical ballads were not included in his collection, because Child felt they were somehow less legitimate than those that

7

seemed to him to be more "ancient." Nineteenth-century authors like Sir Walter Scott and poets like Robert Burns also helped to promote the idea of ballads as being a unique product of the British (or, in their case, Scottish) people. In the wake of the work of Child and other ballad scholars, early folklorists began recording their full text and music, either in notation or on early recording media such as wax cylinders and discs.

Ballads were particularly popular from the mid-eighteenth century in Great Britain, so it's not surprising that the first settlers to come to the United States brought these songs with them. While ballads could be found throughout the original thirteen colonies, the singing tradition seemed to be particularly popular in the Appalachians, where settlers were often cut off from newer forms of music and entertainment. This, at least, was the belief of early collectors, including the British team of Cecil Sharp and Maude Karpeles, who sought out "remnants" of the Child ballads in the Southern mountains. Like many folklorists, they viewed ballad singing as a dying tradition that had to be preserved, with its singers being the last remaining practitioners of what they viewed as an "ancient art." Ironically, every new generation of collectors took a similar view, so that the children, grandchildren, and great-grandchildren of the early ballad singers were also viewed as strange musical "holdouts," whose music had to be preserved before it quickly perished. By the early nineteenth century, ballad singing was a unique part of Southern musical identity, particularly among the mountaineers who scraped out livings working small subsistence farms.

Dance music was another important music form that was brought to the new continent from the British Isles. In the 1700s, London publisher John Playford published what many consider to be the first modern collection of English dance music, along with instructions on how to perform the dances. Traveling dance masters were common throughout the colonies, particularly in

New England, teaching both the music and steps to an eager audience. Tiny portable fiddles—sometimes built into a walking stick—were often used to provide the music, although the popular military instruments of fife and drum—which the American military had introduced during the Revolutionary War years—were also used to accompany dances.

Finally, religious song was brought to America by the Puritan churches. Faced with the prospect of teaching these songs to a largely musically illiterate population, traveling "singing masters" developed a new form of notation, using different shapes to distinguish the different scale tones. Shape-note singing originally arose in New England during the late eighteenth century and then spread to the South and West. Itinerant teachers went from town to town, mostly at the invitation of a local church, to teach the choir how to sing. They employed special songbooks that drew on a repertoire of well-known folk tunes and hymns that were popular in early America. These hymns were often limited to a five-note (pentatonic) scale, which was common to folk tunes. The harmonies were also simplified, based on common intervals such as fourths and fifths, giving the music a distinct, archaic sound. By singing the tones associated with the shapes, the congregation could quickly learn new songs and new harmonies.

Although shape-note singing soon died out in the cities, where more sophisticated congregations learned to read music "properly," it lingered in rural areas. Annual conventions were held with the purpose of singing an entire songbook in a single day and evening (this was accomplished by rapidly "reading" each hymn). This helped singers remember the repertoire and also encouraged them to broaden the number of songs they performed throughout the year. These events would also involve communal socializing, and often a large community-prepared meal would be served about halfway through the day.

Much of this music might never have been known beyond the individual musicians and the local communities where they lived, but at the dawn of the twentieth century, a new breed of folklorists and song collectors arose with the specific mission of documenting "American" music. Like the earlier British collectors, they believed they were helping to preserve music that was unique to their country and that expressed its true values. Key among these collectors were a father-and-son team named John and Alan Lomax.

Born in Goodman, Mississippi, John Avery Lomax was fascinated with the local songs and legends that he heard from his neighbors, family, and friends. He also absorbed many ideas from popular novels and newspapers, which promoted several mythic American figures and ideas. The frontiersman was an established American stereotype, thanks to the hugely popular books by James Fenimore Cooper; translated to the Southwest, a new hero—the cowboy, a lone hero driving cattle across a barren landscape, fighting off hostile natives—was born. While promoted as true-blue Americans, many real cowboys were native Mexican or mestizo (of mixed Spanish and native heritage), known as *vaqueros*, who brought with them their own style of story songs. Like Anglo-American ballads, these songs immortalized the exploits of these hard-working men.

When Lomax entered Harvard, he met folklorist George Lyman Kittredge, a noted collector of folk ballads, who encouraged his students to collect songs. Lomax published his first collection of what he called "cowboy songs" in 1910. A canny promoter, Lomax enlisted naturalist and politician Teddy Roosevelt to write the book's preface. Like other early collectors, Lomax only printed the lyrics to the songs, many of which he had collected either from local newspapers or from correspondents who sent him the words to songs they had heard. Although presented as "authentic," many of these songs were in fact nineteenth-century compositions that greatly sentimentalized the cowboy lifestyle. Lomax's book became the source for many so-called cowboy recording stars from the '30s on, introducing songs that have become veritable chestnuts, such as "Home on the Range."

After working for a while in banking and as a dean at the University of Texas, Lomax returned to his first love, collecting traditional songs. He took to the road in 1933, bringing along one of the first portable recording machines (it recorded on discs and was powered by the battery of his car). His eighteen-year-old son, Alan, accompanied him. While the elder Lomax had many racial prejudices common to his generation, his son was an avowed champion of the people, sympathetic to the Communist Party and its progressive agenda. Alan Lomax would become director of the Library of Congress's Archive of American Folk Song in the late '40s, as well as a prominent spokesperson for traditional music on the radio. He was among the first to recognize the value of early country music recordings when—working in the late 1940s as a consultant to the Decca record label—he produced two collections of 78s that reissued earlier country hits. The Lomaxes published several collections of traditional music—including 1934's *American Ballads and Folk Songs*, 1941's *Our Singing Country*, and 1947's *Folk Song, U.S.A*—featuring the songs' melodies as well as lyrics. In the late '50s, Alan was among the first to take stereo equipment into the field, producing two large series of recordings of traditional country and blues music from the South.

Undoubtedly influenced by his leftist politics, Alan viewed this music as an "authentic expression of the people," as opposed to the pop music of his day, which he thought was produced solely for the profit of commercial interests. He considered the lyrics of many pop songs to be vapid and trite, while folk songs expressed real feelings and documented important events in the life of the country. Ironically, much of the music that Lomax championed had its source in the same commercial music industry as the pop songs he despised—although it was produced decades earlier, so many people failed to make this connection. While Lomax preferred singers like Aunt Molly Jackson—who sang of the struggles in the coal fields and the need for workers to unionize— he didn't ignore music that was purely for entertainment, including the ballads, songs, and dance tunes that he recorded throughout his long career.

African American traditions: Work songs, religious music, and blues

No American musical story is complete without including the rich heritage of music that was brought to this continent through the terrible practice of slavery. Despite many attempts to suppress their music, these transplanted people had a huge impact on American culture. African singing styles, repertory, and approaches to rhythm and performance were all hugely influential beginning as early as the eighteenth century. And, despite prejudice and racism, musicians on both sides of the color line shared ideas that led to the creation of truly American musical styles.

Perhaps because the slaves were brought to this country to perform manual labor—particularly working in the vast cotton fields of the South—their first great contributions to American music were work songs. These songs had many functions: to coordinate the work of a group of people (such as in digging ditches or building a wall), to communicate across a distance, or to express deep emotions or comment on events of the day. Singers brought African characteristics to this new musical style, including flattening of certain notes (later known as "blue notes"), elongating and embellishing certain notes for extra emphasis, and stretching the beat to the point of near stasis.

Slavery was supported by a concerted effort to erase African traditions and replace them with European ones. Nowhere was this stronger than in the practice of religion. Although many

African religious traditions survived (sometimes carefully hidden from the eyes of their white masters), many others were subsumed into European Christianity. By the late nineteenth century, this led to the development of what became celebrated as African American spirituals. Sung using European harmonies and expressing approved religious sentiments, spirituals were admired by both white and black listeners. For whites, they seemed to indicate that the black population had been successfully incorporated into American life—and were happy with their lot as second-class citizens. For black listeners— particularly those who strived toward joining the middle class—the spirituals featured just enough elements of African vocal and rhythmic styles to be identifiably "black," while clothed in an acceptable "white" form. This was no doubt aided by tours of vocal groups associated with the new black colleges that were formed during Reconstruction, most notably the Fisk University Singers from Nashville, who performed in the United States and abroad for white audiences.

Perhaps the musical style most closely associated with African American musicians that developed during the final third of the nineteenth century was the blues. Some believe that this song style combined elements of work songs—particularly those that employed free rhythms to express intense feelings—with the more regular forms introduced through the spirituals. So-called songsters were the main purveyors of this new musical style. These performers sang a range of different types of popular songs and usually performed within a small region, on city streets, in work camps and outside of factories, or any other place people gathered outside of the church. They developed a repertory of songs that commented on current events, true love, and love gone wrong, as well as the hard lot faced by most African Americans. All of these topics would be central to country music as well. Eventually, these songs would be incorporated by more professional songwriters and performers into a more regular form, featuring a fixed harmonic progression and a three- or four-line stanza.

This would become the commercial blues that exploded into popularity in the early '20s.

The beginnings of commercial country music

Just as in other fields, commercial interests entered the entertainment world as new industries—including native music publishing and the opening up of performance spaces in big cities and smaller towns—grew rapidly. As transportation improved, it became possible for professional entertainers to make a living, often traveling with their own tents and other accoutrements so they could stage shows in even the most remote locations. Beginning in the 1830s, a new musical entertainment swept the nation. This first great American popular music—which would become known as minstrelsy—mixed European and African musical traditions. Despite its roots in racist parody, it embodied the kind of musical interchange that would become central to the development of most American popular music styles, including country music. Its white originators freely admitted that they copied the music and performance styles of their black neighbors—and inadvertently opened their countrymen's ears to the lure of syncopated song and dance.

The minstrels used a number of musical instruments, including both melody instruments (ranging from small accordions, known as melodeons, to fiddles) and rhythmic ones (often a pair of animal bones were clacked together to provide a rhythmic accompaniment). But the instrument most closely associated with minstrelsy was the five-string banjo, which many claim to be the first uniquely American musical instrument.

The five-string banjo developed in the mid-nineteenth century and probably derived from earlier West African instruments. Several African instruments with long necks and animal skin–covered bodies have been suggested as its ancestor, and it is likely that features from different earlier instruments helped inspire the banjo's original creators. The use of separate drone and melody strings is another African-influenced feature. However, European instruments like the fiddle and guitar were also influential in its design, particularly in its flat fingerboard, tuning pegs, and drum-like body frame. It may be that leftover Civil War drums were repurposed into serving as banjos; in fact, one of the first known manufacturers of the instrument had previously made drums for the war effort. So, like minstrel music, this characteristic instrument wed European and African culture to create something entirely new.

Early banjos were generally made with wooden bodies and rims, a fretless neck, and a skin head. The original banjo playing style has been variously called clawhammer, frailing, rapping, or knocking. It involves brushing the back of the hand across the strings while catching the thumb on the fifth string. There are many different varieties of clawhammer styles, from highly melodic to highly percussive. This style was refined by the minstrels, who adapted finger-picking techniques from classical guitar playing to the instrument. It's probable that their playing combined various different styles, from the purely rhythmic to a more "genteel" melodic style that was then popular.

White minstrel star Joel Walker Sweeney is generally credited with adding the short fifth or drone string to the banjo. Raised on a Virginia plantation, Sweeney claimed to have learned the instrument from blacks working the fields there. This may have been an attempt to claim a legitimate connection to African American culture; early minstrels often claimed to be "true delineators" of African culture. Nonetheless, Sweeney's most popular songs—including "Lucy Long" and "Such a Getting' Upstairs"—have clear African elements in their melodies and syncopation and undoubtedly in how he performed them.

Just as folk-revival musicians during the late '50s and the '60s would later carry banjos as a sign of their legitimacy as "true" carries of the tradition, minstrels were immediately identified through their association with the banjo. An explosion of banjo manufacturing began in the final decades of the nineteenth century, making the instrument readily available. It became popular among middle-class musicians, and surprisingly, banjo orchestras arose— particularly on Ivy League college campuses—where young men would enjoy playing everything from light classical compositions to the latest ragtime hits. Around the turn of the century, ragtime players like Fred Van Epps and Vess L. Ossmann popularized a picked style; this style is known as "classical" or "ragtime" banjo today. Improved instrument designs helped increase the banjo's popularity. Makers like the Vega Company out of Boston introduced new metal tone rings that helped project the instrument's sound, so it could be heard in a band setting.

Close in popularity to the banjo was the American guitar. Earlier Spanish-style instruments had enjoyed some popularity among the wealthy classes in America, but it took a new group of instrument builders to make the guitar cheaper to produce and more popular among ordinary musicians. Most notable was a German immigrant named Christian Friedrich Martin, who immigrated to New York in the early nineteenth century. Martin didn't enjoy city life and moved to a rural community populated by his fellow countrymen in Pennsylvania. He developed a new guitar design that allowed him to make increasingly larger—and louder—instruments. Originally promoted primarily to young ladies—as an instrument that they could play at home to entertain family members and attract suitors—it spread quickly to traveling performers. The guitar was better suited than the banjo as an accompanying instrument for popular songs.

The guitar and banjo were not the only instruments that were being incorporated by amateur and professional musicians into the new musical styles that were coming together to be the roots of commercial country music. The mandolin—also prominently

1. This tintype shows an amateur duo playing guitar and banjo, photographed around the turn of the twentieth century. Inexpensive musical instruments available through mail order catalogs allowed many would-be performers to start their careers during this period.

played in college orchestras and bands—began to attract players, particularly after instrument maker Orville Gibson developed a new design for the instrument around the turn of the twentieth century. Fiddles were found nearly everywhere, and other members of the violin family, including cellos and basses, were trickling down into family bands. Two types of dulcimer were played: one was a three-string zither that features two drone strings and a melody string that was based on earlier Germanic roots; the other was a larger, multistringed zither that was played with small hammers, which was based on instruments found in a wide variety of cultures, from the British Isles to the Middle East.

While many artists performed in their local towns—and some gained regional success—it's likely that much of this music making would have been lost if it were not for the development of the recording industry. Initially based primarily in New York City, it took a while for recording executives to discover that there was an audience for this—to them—invisible music that was occurring in the country's hinterlands. At first, classical music, Broadway, and vaudeville singers were the primary figures recorded, with records (and machines to play them) being most prevalent in the cities. With the development of more portable machines, which were spring-driven so they did not require electricity to run, records began trickling into more rural areas. Occasionally, a country musician would make his or her way to New York to record; this is how an award-winning Texas fiddler named Eck Robertson was recorded in 1922 for Victor Records, a major recording company of the era. Ironically, Robertson's fiddle style was much more "modern" in approach than many who would record later. Without sales figures, it's impossible to know how well this record sold, but apparently it was not successful enough to encourage Victor's executives at the time—who were mostly focused on their classical recordings of artists like Enrico Caruso—to seek out other country musicians.

Smaller labels were more adventurous, with less to lose and more appetite to discover market niches where they could best a major player like Victor. They also were more responsive to their individual dealers, who could request that they produce custom records for their individual markets. OKeh Records was one such company. Their Atlanta, Georgia, agent contacted the New York office one day in 1923, suggesting that they record a popular local artist named "Fiddlin'" John Carson. OKeh sent their then-director of recording, Ralph Peer, to Atlanta to cut two songs. When Peer heard Carson play, he described his music as "plu-perfect awful." The initial 78 was issued without a label. Yet, on his return to New York, he heard that all 500 copies pressed were sold out in a single day and Atlanta was cabling for more. If Bristol, Tennessee, produced the big bang, Fiddlin' John Carson lit the fuse for what would become a new style of popular music.

2

"Wildwood flowers": Country music goes mainstream, 1923–1930

In discovering a market for country music, the primarily
New York–based recording industry scrambled to record more
"authentic" acts. This involved sending producers to the South;
they relied on leads from local dealers, newspaper announcements,
and word of mouth to produce a string of possible performers.
Thanks to this commercial push, many artists who would not have
had the opportunity otherwise were able to record. A few were
popular enough that they were able to establish, at the minimum,
regional careers. Local radio also pulled from the pool of regional
talent, giving a wide range of musicians who might otherwise
never have played beyond the limits of their hometowns the
chance to make a living from music. This chapter will focus on
some of the best early country stars, from Fiddlin' John Carson to
Lily May Ledford, along with the two best-known acts, the Carter
Family and Jimmie Rodgers.

Fiddlers and string bands

When Georgia-born Fiddlin' John Carson made his first
recordings, he already had decades of experience as a local
entertainer. John held a steady job, working in many different
cotton mills that were located in the Atlanta area, but his real
occupation was fiddle player, storyteller, and singer-raconteur.
He began performing on the streets, selling song sheets of his

original compositions, sometime around 1915. He played for local club meetings, barn dances, and house parties and competed in the many fiddle contests that were held throughout the region, winning many titles through the early '20s. In the days before electrical amplification, John's strong voice and powerful fiddle could cut through the noise of a good-sized crowd.

John first appeared on local station WSB in September 1922, one of the nation's first commercial radio stations. Like many stations, its management came up with a catchy slogan based on its call letters, claiming that "WSB" meant "Welcome South, Brother." Radio, as we shall see, played a key role in the dissemination of country music—as important, if not more important, than the nascent recording industry. His local fame brought him to the attention of Polk Brockman, a furniture dealer and local distributor for OKeh records, who urged the label to record him.

Carson's first recording, "Little Old Log Cabin in the Lane," was a late nineteenth-century popular sentimental song with lyrics that offered a nostalgic vision of country life. On the flip side, John recorded a popular comic fiddle instrumental, "The Old Hen Cackled and the Rooster's Going to Crow," which was undoubtedly one of his "trick" numbers that he used to win many fiddle contests. On it, he imitated the sound of a cackling hen, who was then answered by her eager mate.

Producer Ralph Peer thought little of the recording, until orders poured in for additional discs. Recognizing a potential hitmaker, Peer had Carson come to New York to cut more solos. It was said that his next recording, "You Never Miss Your Mother until She's Gone," sold a million copies, although sales figures are notoriously difficult to verify in this period. This may have been the first country hit to focus on the mother as a symbol of the humble woman devoted to her family, who tried to guide her wayward son away from a life of sin. John would make many more recordings, often accompanied by his laconic partner, "Moonshine Kate" (his daughter Rosa Lee Carson). Kate provided a perfect foil to John's exuberant vocals, providing simple harmony parts and accompanying him on either the banjo or guitar. When string bands became popular, OKeh convinced Carson to put together a larger group, called the Virginia Reelers. The band had great difficulty following John's flexible sense of rhythm.

Recognizing a good thing, the major label Columbia went to Atlanta to find its own fiddling star and discovered another talented old-timer: James Gideon "Gid" Tanner, a local chicken farmer and entertainer. Tanner was Carson's number-one rival on the fiddle contest circuit, and the two alternated taking top honors. Tanner went to New York to record for the label in early 1924, accompanied by a younger, blind guitarist named Riley Puckett. Puckett was an established entertainer in the greater Atlanta area, who made his mark both at fiddlers' meets and on WSB; the local press dubbed him the "Bald Mountain Caruso." Not surprisingly, Columbia had them cover Carson's first hit, "Little Old Log Cabin in the Lane," at this first session. Tanner sang in a comically high falsetto voice, and his fiddle playing was in the rough, often loose rhythmic style typical of his generation of Georgia fiddlers.

In 1926, Columbia urged Tanner to form a band. He invited the younger Georgia fiddler Clayton McMichen to join with him and Puckett, along with banjoist Fate Norris (who can just barely be heard on their recordings), to form the original Skillet Lickers. Influenced by the jazz and pop music of the '20s, McMichen was intent on giving the group a more modern sound. Unlike in other string bands, the banjo was always kept discreetly in the background, perhaps reflecting McMichen's feeling that the instrument was old-fashioned and not suited to his more modern, hard-driving music. Among their popular recordings were traditional dance numbers like "Soldier's Joy" and ragtime-era hits like "Bully of the Town." Their series of comic records, titled "A Corn Licker Still in Georgia," gave the band a chance to play portions of their most popular numbers, alternating with a somewhat stilted, scripted routine.

The third great string band of the period was led by banjo player and vocalist Charlie Poole. Born in rural Randolph County, North Carolina, Poole developed a unique banjo style based on the traditional styles of his region. Poole worked most of his life in the textile mills, as did many other musicians from the area. In the early '20s, he formed the North Carolina Ramblers, originally featuring fiddler Posey Rorer and guitarist Norman Woodlieff. In 1925, the group went to New York to record for Columbia Records. Their first record was "Don't Let Your Deal Go Down," a blues-influenced song that remained in print for years and became Poole's signature number.

The band had a unique style, centering around Poole's wry, uninflected vocal style and intricate, chordal work on the banjo. Poole sang a combination of sentimental "heart" songs (songs that expressed sentimental or nostalgic themes of hearth and home) and comic novelty numbers, many originating in the late nineteenth and early twentieth centuries. Unlike other string bands, the North Carolina Ramblers were a subdued group, focusing on Poole's banjo and vocals, which were accompanied by discreet guitar and fiddle. Poole's versions of many songs, including "Jay Gould's Daughter," "Ramblin' Blues," "Hungry Hash House," and "If I Lose (Let Me Lose)," have become standards in the old-time country repertoire. The band went through several personnel changes over its life, but its sound remained remarkably the same. By 1931, Poole was so popular that he was invited to Hollywood to provide background music for the movies. However, he died of a massive heart attack before he could make the trip West. Years of heavy drinking and hard living had taken their toll on the musician.

Women did not go unrecorded during these early years. Among the female pioneers were Samantha Bumgarner, Eva Davis, and

Roba Stanley, all of whom first recorded in 1924. Fiddler Samantha Bumgarner and guitarist Eva Davis were among the pioneering country stars who made their way to New York City hoping to make a commercial recording. Hailing from Silva, North Carolina, near Asheville, the duo had enjoyed some local success before making the decision to visit Columbia Record's studios, just a month after Tanner and Puckett had made their first 78 there. Bumgarner was the elder musician, then in her mid-forties, and both women played banjo in addition to their main instruments. They cut a number of well-known dance songs, including "Cindy in the Summertime," featuring Bumgarner's rough-hewn fiddle work and Davis's chord work on the banjo. Bumgarner sang some ballads accompanied by her solo fiddle, including a version of the traditional folk ballad "John Hardy," and also cut some of the first banjo songs on record. Yet to recognize a separate market for "old-time" music, Columbia marketed the records as novelties among their regular pop releases. Bumgarner continued to perform in the Asheville area with her neighbor, banjo player Bascom Lamar Lunsford, attracting the attention of folk revivalists as early as the 1940s.

Banjo and guitar player Roba Stanley performed in the Atlanta area, often with her fiddle-playing father and other family members, and had also appeared on WSB. She recorded for OKeh in the same makeshift studio in Atlanta almost a year to the day after John Carson made his first discs. She told country music scholar Charles Wolfe, "There was this one big old room high upstairs in this old building. We sang into this big horn . . . I remember we had to get close to the horn. It was pretty hard work." Her naturally strong voice was perfect for the then-primitive recording technology, and she was able to cut through the background noise. Her best-selling disc was "Darling Nellie Gray," an old minstrel-era hit.

Stanley's success attracted the attention of another early country recording star, Henry Whitter. Born in Fries, Virginia, Whitter supported himself as many others did in the region by working in a cotton mill, while playing music on the side. Like Bumgarner and Davis, Whitter made his way to New York, convincing OKeh records to record his songs and harmonica solos. The guitar player and vocalist scored his first success in 1924 with the railroad ballad "The Wreck of the Southern Old 97." The song memorialized a tragic accident that occurred in Danville, Virginia, in 1903, when a mail train tumbled down a seventy-five-foot ravine, killing several of the trainmen. The song was an immediate bestseller, and other labels rushed to issue their own versions. Its most famous recording was by Vernon Dalhart (1883–1948), who had previously toured as a vaudeville singer. It became country music's first million-selling hit and launched Dalhart as the first nonrural country music star.

Whitter had copyrighted the song in his own name (which led to several later lawsuits), which meant he was among the first country stars to earn royalties from its many recordings. With his unexpected windfall, Whitter was able to treat himself to a brand-new Model T Ford, and he became a local celebrity in his home region. In 1925, he accompanied Roba Stanley on her second recording session, playing guitar and harmonica, just before Stanley married and retired from performing. Two years later, he partnered with West Virginia–born blind fiddler G. B. Grayson, and the duo made several successful records. Grayson was vastly more talented than Whitter, with a smoother singing voice and strong skills as a fiddler. Their repertoire was a typical mixture of dance tunes and minstrel-era and more recent popular songs. Grayson was tragically killed in an auto accident in 1930, and Whitter passed eleven years later.

Radio sweeps the country: The birth of the *National Barn Dance* and the *Grand Ole Opry*

Originally a technological novelty that was first used for communications during World War I, radio revolutionized

American entertainment, much like the Internet would do many decades later. In 1922, the first few commercial stations—like Atlanta's WSB—began broadcasting, and by the mid-'20s radio sets were common and stations proliferated, many operating out of major cities, but with considerable broadcast reach thanks to their powerful transmitters. Hungry for content and looking for anything that would draw listener's ears, these early stations initially featured "high-class" entertainers such as classical musicians and opera singers. But it wasn't long before local talent began to appear on the radio as well, and the number of phone calls and amount of fan mail arriving at the stations ensured that they were added to the programming.

The two longest lasting country music radio programs were Chicago's *National Barn Dance*, begun in 1924, and Nashville's *Grand Ole Opry*. Both were founded by pioneering announcer George Dewey Hay. Born in rural Indiana, Hay was hired as a reporter for the Memphis *Commercial Appeal* in 1920. The paper branched out into the new field of radio and assigned Hay to work as an announcer. At the station, he began to develop his on-air persona, calling himself "The Solemn Old Judge" and opening his broadcasts by tooting on "Hushpuckena," his nickname for the steamboat whistle that became his on-air signature. In 1924, Hay was hired away by WLS (nicknamed by its original owner Sears, Roebuck as "World's Largest Store") in Chicago to be the announcer for their popular *National Barn Dance* program. He gained national exposure on this program and within a year won a popularity poll as the top radio performer in the United States.

In October 1925, the National Life Insurance Company of Nashville opened its radio station, WSM (from "We Shield Millions," the insurance firm's motto). Hay joined the new station as an announcer and newsman. On November 28, 1925, he invited local old-time fiddler Uncle Jimmy Thompson to perform on the station, inaugurating a program Hay called the *WSM Barn Dance*.

"Wildwood flowers"

2. The historic Ryman Auditorium in downtown Nashville was home to the Grand Ole Opry from 1941 to 1974. Built by Thomas Green Ryman as a religious tabernacle in 1892, for years it was the largest auditorium in the South. After the Opry moved to Opryland in 1974, the building was shuttered, but it has since reopened and has once again become a favorite center for country music performance.

In January 1926, the show was renamed, following a famous quip by Hay. The radio station carried the NBC Symphony Orchestra, a program they picked up from New York. When Hay's *Barn Dance* program followed a symphonic broadcast, the announcer said: "You've been up in the clouds with grand opera; now get down to earth with us in a…Grand Ole Opry." The name stuck.

Hay was responsible for booking many of the early *Opry* stars, and he did much to bring the best local talent to the station. Hay formed a WSM Artists Bureau in the 1930s, arranging for tours for many of the radio performers. The success of the *Opry* helped establish Nashville as a center of country music recording and also introduced country music to countless listeners over its long existence.

One of the earliest stars of the *Opry* was "Uncle Dave" Macon. Macon was born outside of Nashville, in Smart Station, Tennessee, but the family soon relocated to the big city, where his father operated a hotel located on its downtown's main street. When Macon was a teenager, his father was killed in a brawl outside of the hotel, and his mother opened a rest stop for stagecoaches in rural Readyville. As a young man, Dave began playing the banjo as a hobby, meanwhile establishing his own freight-carting business, using mule-drawn wagons. However, after several successful years, the arrival of engine-driven trucks began to threaten Macon's business. In his fifties, he decided he could not adapt to new times and let his business go.

Throughout this period, Macon had continued to play the banjo, mostly to amuse his customers and family. In the early '20s, while visiting a Nashville barbershop, Macon was playing for customers when he was heard by a scout for Loew's vaudeville houses. Macon was soon performing on stage, and in early 1924 he made his first recordings. A year later, he was invited to be the second member of WSM's *Grand Ole Opry*.

Macon was an exceptionally talented musician, but it was his ability to perform stunts, like playing the banjo while swinging the instrument between his legs and other tricks he learned through years of informal entertaining, that won over his audiences. Many of his routines had direct roots in the blackface minstrel tradition, and Macon was not averse to singing the "coon songs" that were a direct offshoot of this racist style. Macon's hearty vocals, good humor, and energetic banjo playing influenced an entire generation of musicians, including Stringbean and Grandpa Jones. He recorded hundreds of 78s, often accompanied by the talented McGee brothers and fiddler Sid Harkreader, going under the name the Fruit Jar Drinkers (illegal moonshine liquor was often dispensed in used fruit jars, hence the name).

Another early *Opry* star was DeFord Bailey, an African American harmonica player, who benefited from the fact that radio listeners were oblivious to a performer's color. Bailey was discovered by Nashville physician Dr. Humphrey Bate, also a harmonica player, who was already playing on the radio. Bate brought Bailey to George Hay for an audition, and he was quickly given a prominent spot on the broadcast. For decades, Bailey was the lone African American performer on the program. Bailey's talents on the harmonica were formidable, and besides being hired to perform on the *Opry*, he was among the first artists to be recorded in Nashville in 1928. His famous "Pan American Blues," with its imitations of train whistles and the sound of a speeding freight train, influenced generations of musicians. Sadly, his style grew out of favor and he was phased off the program by 1941. Bailey blamed racism for his failure to build on his career; Hay blamed Bailey for his failure to learn new material. Bailey spent the final decades of his life an embittered man, turning down recording offers and most other opportunities to play. He operated a shoeshine stand in Nashville until his retirement and passed away in relative obscurity.

By the 1930s, both the *National Barn Dance* and *Opry* were moving into more popular music styles, as both were broadcasting at least part of their weekly shows via the national networks; more traditional acts increasingly were given less airtime. A third prominent radio country show premiered in the late '30s as a deliberate throwback to earlier sounds. Spearheaded by producer John Lair, *The Renfro Valley Barn Dance* was as much a stage show as a radio one. Lair particularly promoted female musicians, whom he dressed in old-style gingham dresses and purposely described as "just simple country girls." One of his "discoveries" was banjo and fiddle player Lily May Ledford. The daughter of tenant farmers, Ledford began playing music as a teenager; at age twenty she won a local fiddle contest, attracting Lair's attention. Lair formed a band that he named the Coon Creek Girls with Ledford as its leader, her sister Rosie on guitar, and two other women on bass and fiddle. It was among the first all-female bands and was cannily marketed for its appeal—although not as sex symbols, as later country girl acts would be, but rather for their wholesome, "back-home" personalities. Ledford's biggest hit was "Banjo Picking Girl," an old-time banjo song that she adapted to fit her personality as a female musician. A high point came when the group—now a trio of Lily May, Rosie, and their sister Minnie—played for President Franklin Roosevelt in 1939.

Country's first major stars: The Carter Family and Jimmie Rodgers

The Carter Family was one of the first and most popular country vocal groups, whose unornamented, nasal harmonies, born and bred in rural church music, are probably the closest we can come to a pure Appalachian sound. The group was powered by its ambitious bass singer, Alvin Pleasant "A. P." Carter. A. P. was a master collector of traditional songs, aided in many of his collecting trips by a local African American singer and guitarist named Leslie Riddle. He reworked these songs into pleasant and memorable melodies that became the first country music hits, including "Keep on the Sunny Side," "The Storms Are on the

Ocean," "Wildwood Flower," "Bury Me beneath the Willow," and their best-known song, "Will the Circle Be Unbroken," an adaptation of a shape-note hymn. Riddle's considerable musical skills enabled them to capture the essence of many of these songs without writing them down or recording them to disc.

Although on first listen the group's music may appear rather subdued, there are several elements to their music that reflected influences beyond their folk roots. The group's sophisticated three-part harmonies—perhaps learned by singing in rural church choirs—marked their music as more highly developed than the often-unaccompanied singing traditions found throughout the South. Most important was Maybelle's considerable skills as a guitarist. Where previous guitar players played simple chords to accompany vocals, Maybelle worked out a way of linking her chord changes through playing syncopated short melodies on the bass strings. Some say that she learned this style from Riddle, and certainly elements of traditional blues playing are heard in Maybelle's approach, While others had used a similar technique—Riley Puckett played brief, sometimes rhythmically free bursts of melody between his chords— thanks to the Carter Family's great popularity, Maybelle's style was highly influential on every country guitarist who followed her.

The Carter Family's first and greatest success came while recording under the supervision of Ralph Peer for Victor records from 1927 to 1933. A. P. cannily promoted them as offering "clean" entertainment, suitable for family audiences, unlike the rowdier string bands who were often associated with dance halls and bars that attracted a rougher crowd. The group continued to record through the late 1930s and early '40s, even though A. P. and Sara's marriage dissolved in 1932. The last "original" Carter Family performance took place in 1943.

At the opposite end of the style spectrum was the other major country recording star of the 1920s: James Charles "Jimmie" Rodgers. Born in Meridian, Mississippi, the son of a railroad man,

3. The Carters sold their first self-published songbook through the mail and at performances. The trio posed on the back bumper of their Model T, the same car that they drove to their first recording session in Bristol, Tennessee.

Rodgers worked as a brakeman until tuberculosis cut short his career in 1924. He began performing as a singer–guitarist, working at local tent shows and on the vaudeville circuit. By the mid-'20s, he had joined forces with a string band called the Teneva Ramblers. In 1927, Rodgers and the group auditioned for Ralph Peer in Bristol, Virginia; Peer signed Rodgers as a solo act to Victor Records.

Rodgers's recordings enjoyed immediate success: his first recording of the tune "Blue Yodel" sold a million copies and was followed by countless variants, each given its own number in the series. Rodgers had major hits with songs like "In the Jailhouse Now," a vaudeville favorite that, thanks to his recording, would become a country standard, and "Waiting for a Train." He also recorded with a wide variety of accompanists, even including jazz trumpeter Louis Armstrong. Rodgers's guitar work was fairly simple, although he did incorporate a basic version of Maybelle Carter's bass runs into his strumming. His vocals reflected the influence of popular singers of the era and thus were less ornamented than that of traditional ballad singers, although sharing some of the same nasal qualities.

Victor Records successfully marketed his recordings by promoting Rodgers as "The Singing Brakeman" and "America's Blue Yodeler." Most of his recordings featured Rodgers's distinctive yodeling, a combination of the traditional Swiss vocal style and the blues singing of African Americans. Plagued by tuberculosis, Rodgers performed and toured as widely as possible, but made his greatest impact through his recordings. He made his last recordings in New York in 1933; two days after this final session, on May 26, he died in his hotel room. The death of Jimmie Rodgers only added to his legendary status; like Hank Williams and Elvis Presley after him, Rodgers became a larger-than-life performer after his death, with record sales continuing unabated today.

In some later publicity photos, Rodgers sports a ten-gallon cowboy hat—an indication of a sea change that was occurring in country music's imagery. It's probably thanks to Jimmie's yodeling talents that, ever since, every cowboy singer has adopted this as a signature element of their performances. After Rodgers's death, new stars arose who played on the image of the lone cowboy, the settler of the American West, who spread the American story from sea to shining sea. Artists like Gene Autry and Roy Rogers would define this "Western" wing of country music, introducing an entirely new, popular country style that would have reverberations for decades to come.

"Wildwood flowers."

4. Rare early sheet music for Jimmie Rodgers's big hit, "Blue Yodel No. 5." Most people learned country songs through recordings, not through sheet music, which was oriented toward home pianists.

3

"Back in the saddle again": The birth of the singing cowboy, 1930–1945

The myth of the cowboy as a lone figure who helped tame the American West is rooted in American literature and poetry going back to at least the late nineteenth century. Although there were some "real" singing cowboys, the image of the singing cowboy was cemented by a series of radio and Hollywood stars, beginning with Gene Autry and running through Roy Rogers and female stars like Patsy Montana. Much of this music was popularized over the radio, particularly on Chicago's *National Barn Dance*, which led to pressure on the *Grand Ole Opry* to modernize its sound. A related phenomenon was the rise of the so-called brother acts—notably the Blue Sky Boys—who were inspired by the more modern harmonies of groups like the Sons of the Pioneers and others to create a smoother form of old-time singing. During the mid-1930s, the new musical style known as Western swing combined cowboy image and country instrumentation with big-band stylings through the work of artists like Bob Wills.

Singing cowboy pioneers

Although Western literature has been popular in America since the days of James Fenimore Cooper and Zane Grey (right up to today with Louis L'Amour), it took several radio and record stars of the mid-1930s—who then made the transition to film and eventually television—to solidify the popularity of the singing cowboy.

Among the first was Gene Autry, who transformed the image of the country singer with his introduction of Western costumes and cowboy lore into his performances. The son of a Texas farmer, Autry began his musical career as a member of the church choir, where his grandfather was the preacher. He purchased his first guitar by mail order in his early teens and began playing at local events. Autry began his career imitating the popular style of Jimmie Rodgers, one of country's most beloved performers. His first radio job was singing on Tulsa radio, where he was billed as "Oklahoma's Yodeling Cowboy." In October 1929, Autry went to New York and broke into the recording world. He had his first hit in 1931 with "That Silver Haired Daddy of Mine." This led to a radio contract with the influential and powerful WLS *National Barn Dance*, where he would remain through mid-1934.

In 1934, Autry gained his first movie role in support of cowboy star Ken Maynard in the film *In Old Santa Fe*; the next year, he starred in his first serial. Autry would appear in almost 100 cowboy films, usually accompanied by his horse, Champion. From 1939 to 1956, he starred on radio in "Gene Autry's Melody Ranch," recording dozens of hit Western-flavored songs. These include "Tumblin' Tumbleweeds," "Back in the Saddle Again," and "The Last Roundup." After World War II, Autry enjoyed his last recording success with children's records, including "Rudolf, the Red-Nosed Reindeer" and "Frosty the Snow Man."

Thanks to Autry's fame, the mid- to late 1930s saw a blossoming of cowboy and cowgirl acts, influenced by successful movie serials starring Autry and other "singing cowboys." These so-called horse operas—combining cowboy music with fanciful plots of the "old West"—were hugely popular, because they reinforced images of a simpler, happier time when good guys wore white and bad guys were always successfully run out of town. Groups like the Sons of the Pioneers and the Girls of the Golden West were two of many that exploited the cowboy imagery and repertory. These bands took popular vocal harmony styles and wed them to cowboy themes. The Pioneers were particularly important, thanks to their handsome lead vocalist, Roy Rogers.

Probably taking his stage name from the recently passed Jimmie Rodgers (although dropping the "d"), Roy Rogers (b. Leonard Slye) was the son of migrant farm workers. His family came to California in 1930 to work as fruit pickers. Roy formed the Pioneer Trio, along with guitarist/vocalist Bob Nolan and vocalist Tim Spencer, to play local jobs. The group became the Sons of the Pioneers around 1934 with the addition of the talented Farr Brothers on guitar and fiddle. With a swinging, jazzy sound and pop-flavored, three-part harmonies, the Pioneers were an immediate sensation on stage and screen. Their big break came supporting Gene Autry in his 1935 film, *Tumbling Tumbleweeds*. Slye decided he could be a singing cowboy, too, and took the names Dick Weston and finally Roy Rogers, leaving the Pioneers around 1937 (although the group continued to appear on film with him). He began starring in B Westerns in 1938 and, four years later, when Autry went off to fight in World War II, became the country's leading cowboy star.

Although Rogers had a pleasant-enough voice, he became more famous as a cowboy actor than a singer. In 1947, he wed Dale Evans, a pop singer who had appeared in many of his Westerns and would continue to work with him throughout the rest of his career. From the '50s until Rogers's death, the pair worked on radio, films, and TV. Their best-known song was their theme song, "Happy Trails." The duo founded their own museum in Victorville, California, where you can visit the stuffed remains of Roy's favorite horse, Trigger.

While Rogers became a major star on his own, the core group of Nolan, Spencer, and the Farrs stuck together as the Pioneers through the early 1950s, playing with various additional members. Spencer was a virtual one-man hit-making machine, creating such classic cowboy songs as "Cool Water," the band's unofficial theme song, "Tumbling Tumbleweeds," and the immortal "A Cowboy Has to Sing"; Spencer was also a prolific songwriter, turning out "Cigarettes, Whiskey, and Wild Women" and "Roomful of Roses." The Sons popularized smooth, harmonized vocals and showy yodeling and performed cowboy rope tricks and other novelties in their stage show.

Another Jimmie Rodgers–influenced performer who took on a cowboy image was Jimmie Davis. Born to a family of sharecroppers, Davis eventually earned a master's degree and taught college for a while during the mid-1920s. Because of his country roots and his pleasant voice, he was invited to sing "old-time" songs in the late '20s by a radio station out of Shreveport, Louisiana, leading to a performing and recording career. Like Autry, Davis sang a mix of sentimental "heart" songs and bluesy numbers. Davis took on a singing cowboy image in 1934, scoring a hit with "Nobody's Darlin' but Mine." He is best remembered today for his 1940 song, "You Are My Sunshine." Unlike Autry and Rogers, Davis was never a major cowboy film star, but he did become a successful politician, running for governor of Louisiana in 1944 and serving for one term and then returning to the governor's office in 1960.

"I Want to Be a Cowboy's Sweetheart": The rise of the cowgirl singer

Women were not to be left out of the cowboy craze. Perhaps the first to ride this wave was singer Patsy Montana, another star of the WLS *National Barn Dance* and a talented fiddler, vocalist, and yodeler. She originally partnered with Jimmie Davis in the early '30s before joining the Prairie Ramblers, a four-piece Western band. Their 1935 recording of "I Wanna Be a Cowboy's Sweetheart" became Montana's million-selling, signature song and laid the groundwork for the success of women in country music after World War II.

5. This is a typical cowboy-themed sheet music cover featuring Patsy Montana. The illustrator included just about every Western cliché he could in the background, including cowpokes in full regalia, horses, and a vaguely Spanish-style promenade.

Another popular female cowgirl featured on the *National Barn Dance* was Louise Massey, who led the group the Westerners. Massey was born in Hart County, Texas, so had some claim to a cowboy heritage. Her family relocated when Massey's father purchased a farm in the then sparsely populated new state of New Mexico in 1914. The entire family of father, mother, and eight children were musically inclined, with dad an old-style Western fiddler and daughter Louise a talented pianist and vocalist. Louise married bass player Milt Mabie in 1919, and he quickly joined the family's musical group. The Massey family band began performing on the local vaudeville circuit in the early 1920s. After the elder Massey retired because of the rigors of life on the road, the rest of the band settled into a five-year stint on KMBC radio out of Kansas City. In 1933, a talent scout for the WLS *National Barn Dance* out of Chicago heard the group and signed them to this influential show.

The center of attention of the band was the glamorous Louise, who besides providing lead vocals was also something of a fashion plate, with her sequined outfits (also worn by the other members of the band) and satin boots. Like most of the cowboy bands of the day, the group played a wide range of material, mostly filtered through a soft, pop sound. Besides the obligatory cowboy and sentimental numbers, they could play dance music from fiddle tunes to Eastern European polkas, waltzes, and schottisches, as well as novelty numbers, ragtime, and light jazz. Louise wrote many of the group's hits, including their early 1934 disc "When the White Azaleas Start Blooming," featuring her honey-voiced vocals, and their biggest hit, 1941's "My Adobe Hacienda," later a crossover country and pop hit after the Second World War. In 1948, Louise and husband Milt retired to New Mexico. Brother Curt went to Hollywood, where he would gain fame as the writer of two of the most memorable TV themes of all time, for *The Beverly Hillbillies* and the spinoff series, *Petticoat Junction*. (That's him singing the *Petticoat Junction* theme song.)

A new era at the Opry

The success of the cowboy singers with their pop-flavored harmonies had an impact on one of Nashville's most venerated institutions, the *Grand Ole Opry*. While originally focusing on "old-time" country performers, the show's producers were aware of the great success of Chicago's *National Barn Dance* and its promotion of younger and more pop-influenced acts like Gene Autry. Its management brought in new producer Harry Stone, who was hired to book more modern acts on the show. In 1931, he brought the Vagabonds, a vocal trio who had previously appeared on the Chicago program. The trio's smooth harmonies and repertoire of popular songs were well received by the *Opry*'s audiences, influencing other acts to modernize their style. In the mid-'30s, cowboy-styled acts like Pee Wee King's Golden West Cowboys appeared on the program, and in 1938, a young fiddler and vocalist named Roy Acuff was invited to join the show. Acuff changed the direction of the *Opry* from being primarily an instrumental broadcast to one focusing on vocals. A year later, the *Opry* joined the NBC network, bringing it to a national audience, and future bluegrass star Bill Monroe joined the cast.

Born to a middle class family in Maynardville, Tennessee, as a teenager Acuff originally hoped to be a professional ballplayer. However, a case of severe sunstroke left him bedridden for two years, during which time he took up the fiddle. He formed his first band in the early 1930s, performing on Knoxville radio. Acuff enjoyed his first hits, "The Great Speckled Bird" and "The Wabash Cannonball," in 1936 and made his first appearance on the *Grand Ole Opry* two years later, where he became a major new star. His last big hit, "Wreck on the Highway," came in 1942. Acuff's vocal style was influenced by crooners like Bing Crosby, and his band introduced the forerunner of the "crying steel guitar" in the work of "Bashful" Brother Oswald, who played the dobro, an acoustic guitar with a metal resonator that was played Hawaiian style, using a steel bar. Acuff became a mover and shaker in Nashville's music community, forming a music publishing partnership with songwriter Fred Rose, which would become the major publisher of country songs. He even ran (unsuccessfully) for governor in his home state in 1948.

In 1940, the *Opry* cast was invited to appear in a movie produced by budget studio Republic Pictures. Acuff, young and handsome, was cast as the lead, but the film also showcased older stars like Uncle Dave Macon. That same year, Eddy Arnold joined the show's cast as featured singer with Pee Wee King. In the summer of 1940, the first *Opry* tent show hit the road, and country comic Minnie Pearl made her debut on the radio program. Pearl's country rube character—dressed in thrift store dresses and hats still carrying their price tags—became one of country's most beloved personalities. She introduced her comic monologues with a lusty "How-dee!," telling stories of her fictional home of Grinder's Switch. Her comic style and persona were models for dozens of future "rube" comedians and would be emulated by the popular public-radio host, Garrison Keillor, on his long-running *A Prairie Home Companion* radio show.

Brothers in harmony

During the 1930s, vocal harmony groups, such as the Sons of the Pioneers and the even more modern-styled Vagabonds (who were featured on the *Grand Ole Opry*), spread a new, smoother singing style to country performance. Several local acts picked up on this harmony singing and incorporated it into their own shows. Not being able to support a full band, many formed duos so they could at least incorporate vocal harmony into their acts. In many cases, these duos consisted of siblings and so came to be known as "brother acts." Among the most successful in this period were the Bolick brothers (known as the Blue Sky Boys) and the Monroe Brothers.

Bill and Earl Bolick were raised in the mountainous western region of North Carolina on a small family farm. They learned their repertoire of traditional songs from family members, gospel hymns from the local church, and sentimental songs from the recordings of 1920s country artists. Bill played the mandolin and taught his younger brother, Earl, to play the guitar. After

6. The Blue Sky Boys were a tremendously popular brother duo, featuring Bill (mandolin) and Earl Bolick (guitar). At the beginning of their career, they appeared on radio and in live shows with fiddler Homer Sherrill.

performing on radio in Asheboro, North Carolina, in the early '30s, the boys were signed to a recording contract in 1936, enjoying immediate popularity. Among their hits were the sentimental favorites "The Sweetest Gift (A Mother's Smile)" and "Short Life of Trouble," along with the more upbeat "Sunny Side of Life" and "Are You from Dixie?," their radio theme song. They wowed their audiences with their carefully arranged vocals, often featuring rapid back-and-forth vocals by the brothers followed by perfectly coordinated harmonies.

A more dynamic duo was made up of Charlie and Bill Monroe. The Monroe family hailed from rural Rosine, Kentucky. Brother Charlie played guitar, Birch played the fiddle, and youngest brother Bill played mandolin. Charlie and Birch left home searching for employment in the North in the mid-1920s, settling in East Chicago, Indiana. Bill joined them there when he was eighteen years old, staying for five years. They worked in the local oil refineries by day, while playing music at nights and on weekends. In 1934, Chicago radio station WLS offered them full-time employment; Birch quit the group, but Charlie and Bill continued as the Monroe Brothers. In 1936, the brothers made their first recordings. They recorded traditional songs and hymns, including their first hit, "What Would You Give (In Exchange for Your Soul)." Their recording of the folk standard "Nine Pound Hammer (Roll on Buddy)" was widely imitated and shows how they could take a traditional song and modernize and energize it. Charlie's laconic delivery was a good foil to his brother's highly charged tenor vocals, and their records and radio appearances were very successful. Bill's mandolin work was revolutionary; rather than simply strumming and playing fills between choruses, he added high-speed licks and a distinctive backbeat "chop" that propelled the music forward. In 1938, the duo split, with each brother forming his own group; Bill would go on to become a pioneer in bluegrass music, as we will see.

A cowboy's gotta swing

As the cowboy singers crossed over to mainstream popularity, their accompaniments changed from prominently featuring fiddles and guitars to incorporating more "modern" pop instruments like accordion, electric steel guitar, and even bass and drums. Thus began country music's relentless push to gain popularity through emulating the sounds and styles of mainstream pop. Meanwhile, a new musical style that blended old-time fiddle tunes with jazz rhythms and instrumentation was developing in the late 1920s in the Texas/Oklahoma region that would become known as Western swing. There, musicians were influenced by blues and jazz recordings, as well as early pop crooners, to form an amalgam of traditional country sounds with a swinging accompaniment.

The band credited with creating this sound was the Light Crust Doughboys. The group was formed in the early 1930s by Burrus

Mills, the makers of Light Crust Flour, to promote their products on radio and through local appearances. The company's public relations man, W. Lee "Pappy" O'Daniel, served as the emcee and used their popularity on radio as a launching pad for his later political career. O'Daniel was a tough taskmaster, paying his musicians poorly and working them very hard, leading many of them to strike out on their own. Two of the group's founding members—vocalist Milton Brown and vocalist and fiddler Bob Wills—were among the first to leave, forming their own highly influential bands.

Milton Brown formed one of the first and hottest bands in Western swing, the Musical Brownies, in 1934. The band featured a swinging fiddler, a jazz-styled pianist, and legendary steel guitarist Bob Dunn, whose rapid-fire, staccato bursts of sound were unequaled at the time. Dunn is said to have been the first player to use an electric instrument on a country recording, and certainly his unique playing style made the instrument stand out. The group further capitalized on this novelty by doubling the fiddle lead with the steel guitar, an effect that would be imitated on other Western swing and later country recordings. The band's repertoire was heavy on blues, jazz, and pop standards, with the occasional country number thrown in. They avoided ballads, perhaps because they worked primarily as a dance band and probably also because Brown's vocal style, a combination of Cab Calloway–style jive and Bing Crosby–style croon, was ill-suited to slower numbers. When Brown died in a car accident on April 18, 1936, his brother, guitarist Durwood, managed to keep the band going for a few years, but most of the key members soon defected to other outfits or to lead their own ensembles.

Fiddler and singer Bob Wills was the son of an old-time fiddler and cotton farmer, who introduced his son to the traditional fiddle tunes of the Southwest. While growing up in rural Texas, Wills worked alongside black laborers in the cotton fields, who sang traditional hollers and blues. Wills absorbed all of these musical influences, as well as the new jazz sounds that he heard on records and radios. Wills left the Doughboys in 1934 to form his own band, the Texas Playboys, and a year later they gained a recording contract.

Wills's new band was defined by two distinctive elements: the newly introduced electric "steel" guitar and the smooth vocalizing of singer Tommy Duncan. Steel guitarist Leon McAuliffe was responsible for the group's big hit, "Steel Guitar Rag"; his burbling solos were a trademark of the early Wills's recordings, and his solos were often introduced by Wills's high falsetto shout of "Take it away, Leon!" McAuliffe's playing was far more mellow than that of his main rival, Bob Dunn, who preferred a much more metallic tone and sharp attack. Tommy Duncan blended a mainstream sensibility with an affinity for the blues of Jimmie Rodgers. The band also featured the fine boogie-influenced piano playing of Al Stricklin and a loping bass-and-drum rhythm section that predicted the shuffle beat of later country boogie outfits. Wills was also a talented songwriter, whose most notable composition was "San Antonio Rose," although he also transformed several traditional fiddle tunes ("Liza Jane," "Ida Red," and others) into swinging, pop confections. By the end of the '30s, the group had grown to include a large brass section, rivaling the popular big bands of the day in size and sound.

World War II spelled the end of the big bands of the 1930s, and Wills turned to working with a smaller outfit out of his new home, Southern California, where he moved to appear in a number of forgettable Hollywood Westerns. Singer Tommy Duncan was expelled from the ranks in 1948 and was replaced by a series of lead vocalists, male and female, who were similarly modern in their approach. The pared-down Wills's band made an excellent series of recordings for MGM in the late 1940s and early '50s that in many ways were more exciting than his big-band sides of the late '30s.

Wills continued to work and record sporadically through the '50s and '60s, most notably recording two reunion LPs with singer

Tommy Duncan in 1961 and 1962. Championed by country performer Merle Haggard, who made a tribute LP to Wills in 1970, he came out of semiretirement in 1973 to supervise one last session, just before suffering a debilitating stroke.

Different Texas Playboys continued to perform in the 1970s and '80s, with one band led by Leon McAuliffe and another led by Wills's brother, Johnnie Lee, who recorded the original version of "Rag Mop" in 1950 (later a hit for the Mills Brothers). Another brother, Billy Jack, worked as a drummer, bassist, and vocalist for Bob's band before forming his own group in 1949. It had the most progressive sound of any of the Western bands, with a jazz and R&B bent that was rarely heard in Western swing.

A second wave of Western swing developed in the late 1940s in Southern California, where many Western musicians had settled after the war. Most successful was a band led by fiddler and vocalist Spade Cooley. Born in rural Oklahoma, Cooley was descended from two generations of fiddle players, so it's not surprising that he played at his first dance at the age of eight. His family relocated from Oklahoma to Southern California during the Depression, where the young Cooley performed with Western-flavored groups.

In the early '40s, Cooley formed his first band, and by the end of World War II they were permanently installed in a Santa Monica ballroom, drawing several thousand cowboy-swing fans a night. Cooley's classic first band featured vocalist Tex Williams, as well as Joaquin Murphey's hot steel guitar and Johnny Weiss's guitar leads, which were reminiscent of jazz great Charlie Christian. In 1943, they recorded Cooley's composition "Shame, Shame on You," with Williams on lead vocals, which would be his biggest hit and become his theme song. Cooley's demanding personality led the entire band, along with singer Williams, to quit in 1946 and go out on their own as the Western Caravan.

In 1948, Cooley was given his own variety show on a local Los Angeles TV station, where he introduced country comic Hank Penny. In the 1950s, Cooley's bands grew in size, sometimes numbering over a dozen members, including full string sections, harp, and accordion, and he slowly gravitated toward a more pop-sounding style. Increasing problems with alcohol led to a decline in his popularity later in the decade, and his personal problems came to a head in 1961 when he shot and killed his wife in front of their teenage daughter. Cooley spent the '60s in prison. He was released to perform at a benefit concert on November 23, 1969; following his performance, he died backstage of a heart attack.

Although many Western swing bands featured female vocalists from time to time, it was rare for a band to center on a female lead. The Maddox Brothers and Rose, another California-based band, was a rare exception to this rule. Originally from Boaz, Alabama, the Maddox family immigrated to Southern California in search of a better way of life in the early 1930s. In later years, Rose recalled how they came to "the Land of Milk and Honey":

> Cotton prices failed in Alabama. So we left for California, the Land of Milk and Honey.... We only had $35 when we left [home].... We got to Los Angeles, California, in 1933.... We lived in Pipe City. There were these huge culvert pipes and all the migrants were living inside culverts. The mayor of Pipe City gave us his pipe to stay in.

In California, Rose's five older brothers formed a band in a Western/cowboy style to perform at local rodeos and parties. In 1937, the group was approached by a Modesto, California, radio station to put on a cowboy music show, with the stipulation that they have a female singer. Twelve-year-old Rose was enlisted, and the group was christened the Maddox Brothers and Rose.

The band temporarily broke up during World War II, but regrouped in the late 1940s, producing a series of high-energy recordings melding Western swing with early honky-tonk.

Rose's big-throated vocals were ably accompanied by the band, along with her brothers' good-natured horseplay. The group's biggest hit was a 1946 cover of Jack and Woody Guthrie's "Philadelphia Lawyer," introducing the song to the country repertoire. The band was featured on the popular *Louisiana Hayride* radio program in the early 1950s and continued to record and perform through 1957.

Rose switched to Capitol Records in 1959 as a solo artist and continued to have hits through the early '60s with her gutsy recordings of "Down, Down, Down," "Sing a Little Song of Heartache," and duets with Buck Owens, another Southern California–based star, notably on the classic "Mental Cruelty." In 1963, bluegrass musician Bill Monroe suggested to her record label that Rose's style was perfectly suited to his style of music, and since the folk revival was in full swing, the label decided to release an album of Rose singing bluegrass standards. This album became a collector's item a decade later during the bluegrass revival and helped launch an entirely new career for Maddox in the 1970s.

The Western swing groups were in the vanguard of introducing key themes into country music—partying and drinking, loving and cheating, and heartbreak and loneliness—that would come to the fore after World War II in a new style that would become known as honky-tonk music. Singers like Ernest Tubb, Eddy Arnold, and most notably Hank Williams would bring increased attention to the solo singer/guitarist as country idol. Meanwhile, women— often despairingly portrayed as evil temptresses who led good men astray—didn't sit idly by; singers like Kitty Wells responded vigorously to this new male-dominated music, establishing an important place for women at country music's table. And, as in many periods where country music was absorbing influences from the pop world, there was some pushback among performers and the audiences, leading to recreations of earlier sounds and styles.

4

"Honky-tonkin'": Postwar country music, 1945–1959

After World War II, the country that American veterans returned to was much changed. The United States was now a major economic and political force on the world stage, and industrialization was occurring throughout the country, transforming even the more remote areas of the South. The displacement of people from rural farms to urban factories led to both a wider spread of country music and a nostalgia for the life left behind. The honky-tonk—a bar featuring either live music or the newly introduced jukebox—became a center of entertainment for men in search of companionship. New subject matter—cheatin', drinkin', and fightin'—replaced older themes of home and family. New stars expressed these themes, including Ernest Tubb, Hank Williams, and George Jones. Female performers also came to the fore, notably Kitty Wells and later Patsy Cline, bringing a different perspective to the changing culture.

Another development in the postwar years was a new approach to string-band music, absorbing many of the innovations of Western swing, honky-tonk, and other musical styles. It would become known as bluegrass, and its main creator, Bill Monroe, would establish a sound that would continue to enjoy popularity many decades later. In the mid-1950s, a major new style arrived on the scene through the recordings of a young, white truck driver from Memphis, Tennessee: Elvis Presley. His outrageous performance style and energetic music influenced a new style, which became known as rockabilly. Meanwhile, a nostalgic backlash, in the form of folk-styled songs and performers who recalled earlier traditions, was conveyed in the work of stars like Marty Robbins and Jimmie Driftwood.

"Walkin' the Floor over You": The birth of honky-tonk

The thousands of soldiers returning from World War II—many of whom had previously never been more than a dozen miles from their hometowns—were joined by workers who had been drawn by the war effort to major cities to work in new factories. Traditional family structures, courtship rituals, and social mores were seriously upended, and in their wake, new gathering places where people could meet and interact had to be developed. The honky-tonk—a small bar often located on the outskirts of town or on the "wrong side of the tracks"—became a center of musical creation. Employing hundreds of smalltime performers (many of whom would later become big-time stars), these local watering holes nurtured a new style of music that would become, in the late 1940s and early '50s, country music's mainstream voice.

Earlier in the century, country musicians had performed at local gatherings, often sponsored by schools or churches, and played for a mixed audience, including women and children. For this reason, their repertoire tended to emphasize mainstream values: religion, home, and faithfulness to one's wife and mother. This strong moralistic tone reached its apex in the songs of the brother acts of the '30s, who popularized songs like "The Sweetest Gift (A Mother's Smile)" and "Make Him a Solider."

Honky-tonks came to the fore in response to the end of Prohibition during the early years of the Great Depression. However, because Southern towns tended to be conservative, and drinking was still frowned upon, these bars tended to be located either on the outskirts of town or in the no man's land between towns. Here, men could gather after work to enjoy a few beers, play pool, and listen to music, which was often provided by a lone guitar player who was barely audible above the racket. For this reason, newly introduced electrified instruments (such as the steel guitar in the '30s and electric guitars and basses in the '50s) and drums became necessary equipment for the smalltime country band, along with microphones to amplify vocals.

Besides this change in presentation, the subject matter of church, mother, wife, and home was hardly appropriate for a rough bar atmosphere. Songwriters responded by creating lyrics that reflected the realities of honky-tonk life. Songs about drifting husbands, enticed into sin by the "loose women" who gathered in bars and the subsequent lyin', cheatin', and heartbreak created by their "foolin' around," became standard honky-tonk fare, particularly in the late '40s. Songs like "Dim Lights, Thick Smoke (and Loud, Loud Music)" celebrate the honky-tonk lifestyle, while at the same time take a moralistic tone, warning against the allure of cheap drinks and equally cheap women. Typically, in the world of country music, the "fallen women" were often blamed for dragging down their hapless "victims," the hard-working country men.

While the original country music radio shows soldiered on, a new show begun during the postwar years gained in popularity by riding the new honky-tonk wave. The show was born in 1948 when Dean Upson, a past talent coordinator for the *Grand Ole Opry*, joined forces with the management of Shreveport, Louisiana's, KWKH to create *The Louisiana Hayride*. The show was given an enormous boost in August 1948 when singer–songwriter Hank Williams joined the roster. Williams, like many after him, stayed only a little over a year before moving to the more prestigious *Opry*. A number of other stars got their start on the station, including Slim Whitman, Webb Pierce, Johnny Horton, and Jim

Reeves. In an ironic twist, Hank Williams returned to the *Hayride* in 1952 after he was fired from the *Opry* due to his drunkenness, but by this time his performances were pretty erratic in quality (he died on New Year's Day, 1953). The show's heavy reliance on younger singers—mostly working in the honky-tonk style—gave this new music a huge boost.

One of the first performers to ride this new wave was Ernest Tubb. Born in the small town of Crisp, Texas (south of Dallas), Tubb had no ambitions to be a country singer until he heard the recordings of Jimmie Rodgers. He was so determined to emulate Rodgers's style that he sought out the singer's widow, who gave him her blessing to perform the Blue Yodeler's material. From the mid-1930s through the early '40s, Tubb honed his style, slowly transforming himself into a more modern, honky-tonk singer. Undoubtedly, his experience performing in many small barrooms across Texas helped shape his newer sound and style, which relied on amplified instruments to cut through the noise, and that expressed classic barroom sentiments.

The real change came with his enormous 1941 hit, the loping "Walking the Floor over You." It was the quintessential honky-tonk anthem (it would become his lifelong theme song) and perhaps the first country recording to feature electric-guitar lead. Tubb's bone-dry delivery, wed with the chunky rhythm of the backup band, made this recording a country classic. During the World War II years, Tubb migrated to Hollywood, where he appeared in several of the era's low-budget cowboy films; he even recorded with pop music's Andrews Sisters.

Tubb made his most influential recordings and radio appearances in the late 1940s and early to mid-1950s with his band, the Texas Troubadours, always featuring electric lead guitar. He nurtured the talents of several guitarists and introduced the electric guitar to the *Opry* when he became a member in 1943. Four years later, he opened his record store down the street from the show's auditorium and for many years hosted WSM's *Midnight Jamboree* radio show, broadcast immediately following the *Opry*, from his store.

But if we must credit honky-tonk's popularity to a single figure, that person is Hank Williams. In songs like "Honky Tonkin'," he contributed a more upbeat, less moralistically dour view of the world of small, seedy bars; his backup combo of crying steel guitar and scratchy fiddle became the model for thousands of honky-tonk bands. Born King Hiram Hank Williams in rural Mount Olive, Alabama (outside of Birmingham), Williams's family were poor dirt farmers who relocated to metropolitan Greenville. Here, Williams first heard the blues performed by street-singer Rufus Payne; like many other white country artists, Williams's life was changed by this exposure to traditional black music. Around 1937, the family moved to Montgomery, where Williams made his first public appearance, leading to a regular spot on local radio. He formed his first band, the Drifting Cowboys, a name that he would use for his backup band throughout his career. He also composed "Six More Miles (to the Graveyard)," a blues tune that for the first time displayed his unique sense of gallows humor.

The war years were spent in Mobile, Alabama, shipyards; during that time, Williams returned to music with a new band, featuring a young female singer, Audrey Sheppard Guy, who was to become his first wife (and mother of Hank Williams Jr.). Williams signed with Nashville music publisher Fred Rose, who became the mastermind behind his successful career, in 1946. After a brief stint with the small label Sterling, Williams signed with MGM in 1947, charting with his first release, the bluesy and ballsy "Move It on Over," and his first honky-tonk anthem, "Honky Tonkin'." Williams could even transform religious-themed material into his own unique style, making a hit out of his own version of "I Saw the Light." In August 1948, Williams joined the *Louisiana Hayride*, which spread his sound throughout the southwest and helped

7. Hank Williams, with his wife Audrey (to his right) and the Drifting Cowboys, broadcast on WSM. Audrey toured and performed with her hard-living husband, perhaps to keep an eye on him on the road.

propel his cover of the 1920s novelty number "Lovesick Blues" into a number-one country hit in 1949.

Williams suffered from severe back problems (possibly spina bifida), leading to terrible back pain for which he self-medicated with alcohol and painkillers. Nonetheless, he continued to turn out major country hits through the remaining three years of his life. The savvy Rose also peddled Williams's songs to more mainstream performers, so that his "Cold, Cold Heart" was a hit for Tony Bennett, "Hey Good Lookin'" scored for Frankie Laine, and Jo Stafford made a hit out of the Cajun novelty number "Jambalaya."

By mid-1952, hard drinking and drug use caught up with the star. He was expelled from the *Opry* and his marriage ended in divorce. He died in the back of a car en route to a performance on New Year's Day in 1953. As often happens, his death propelled his final recordings, "Your Cheatin' Heart" and the novelty "Kaw-Liga," to the top of the country charts. Like many other performers who died young, Williams's death cast a long shadow. His recordings have been in print continuously since his death.

The honky-tonk style reached its apex in Hank Thompson's 1952 recording of "The Wild Side of Life," another song that both celebrates and criticizes the honky-tonk life. Henry William Thompson was born in Waco, Texas. During his teen years, he performed on local radio under the name of "Hank the Hired Hand," as well as recording for the tiny, local Globe label. These sides were so successful that they led Tex Ritter to recommend him to California-based Capitol Records, which signed the singer in 1948, where he remained for eighteen years. His backup band, the Brazos Valley Boys, featured the drive of a good Western swing outfit; on record and tours, they were often augmented by legendary guitarist Merle Travis. While the band was swinging in orientation, Thompson's song choice focused on women, booze, and heartbreak—classic honky-tonk themes.

Thompson's first big hit was "Humpty Dumpty Heart" from 1948; he followed this with many classics, including 1952's honky-tonk theme song, "Wild Side of Life." In the mid-1950s, he helped promote singer Wanda Jackson by featuring her in his live shows and in recordings. In the early '60s, impressed by the success of big-band vocalist Louis Prima, who had established a successful career in Las Vegas, Thompson began regularly performing there as well, recording a fine live LP in Vegas in 1961.

While many honky-tonk performers were men—and the songs they sang were from a male point of view—this doesn't mean that there weren't female singers who rose to the challenge. Most notably, Thompson's "Wild Side of Life" inspired the wonderful answer song, "It Wasn't God That Made Honky Tonk Angels," which made a major star out of Kitty Wells. Born Muriel Deason in Nashville, Wells began performing on local radio with her siblings as the

Deason Sisters in 1936. A year later, she wed Johnnie Wright, a talented musician. Soon after, she began performing with Johnny along with her sister-in-law, Louise Wright, as Johnnie Wright and the Harmony Girls. In 1939, Johnnie added Jack Anglin (who had married Louise) to the band to form the Tennessee Hillbillies (later the Tennessee Mountain Boys). In 1942, Jack was drafted, so Johnny began performing with his wife as a duo; at this time, he christened her "Kitty Wells," taking her stage name from the folk ballad "Sweet Kitty Wells." After the war, Jack reunited with Johnny to form the popular country duo Johnnie and Jack. In 1948, they joined the new *Louisiana Hayride* show, which made their reputation, winning them a contract with RCA.

In 1949, Kitty began recording gospel numbers backed by Johnnie and Jack's band, with little success. Meanwhile, the duo's recordings sold well. Semiretired as a housewife, Kitty was lured back into the studio for one more try at recording in 1952. Paul Cohen, a Decca label executive, wanted her to record a woman's answer song to the immensely popular "Wild Side of Life." "It Wasn't God That Made Honky Tonk Angels" rightfully asserted that men had to share the blame for the "fallen women" who frequented the rough-and-tumble backwoods bars. The song shot up the country charts, establishing Wells's popularity. Through the '50s and '60s, Wells proved she was no one-hit wonder. On solo recordings ("I Can't Stop Loving You," "Mommy for a Day," "Heartbreak U.S.A.") and duets with Red Foley ("One by One," "As Long as I Live"), she honed her image as the gutsy good girl, unafraid to express a woman's point of view.

Bill Monroe and the birth of bluegrass

Alan Lomax famously called bluegrass "folk music with overdrive," leading some to caricature it as high-speed, high-pitched, high-energy music. Taking its name from the legendary band led by mandolinist Bill Monroe in the late 1940s, bluegrass is much more than just fancy pickin' and breathless singing. It is a music of great emotional power that borrows from country, gospel, honky-tonk, and, more recently, jazz and rock to form a unique musical union.

All bluegrass bands owe a debt to Bill Monroe, who brought together a group of five musicians to form the first classic lineup of his Blue Grass Boys in 1946. These included Lester Flatt and Earl Scruggs on lead guitar/vocals and banjo, respectively, fiddler Chubby Wise, Monroe on mandolin and high tenor vocals, and bass player Cedric Rainwater. Scruggs had evolved a unique method of playing the five-string banjo, a three-finger picking style that changed the instrument from primarily an accompaniment to a melodic lead instrument. Flatt developed a new way of playing guitar accompaniments, using bass runs rather than chords as "fills" to bridge the gaps between chord progressions. Monroe was, of course, a master mandolin player, and Wise was a fiddler influenced as much by Western swing as he was by old-time styles. Vocally, the group offered a strong contrast between the relaxed, almost crooning lead vocals of Flatt with the intense, high-pitched harmonies and leads of Monroe. It is not an exaggeration to say that Monroe's band—vocally and instrumentally—not only invented bluegrass, but also became the model that every other band has emulated.

Through their appearances on the *Grand Ole Opry* and on record in the late '40s, Monroe's group had an immediate and revolutionary impact on other string bands. Bands like the Stanley Brothers, who had been playing in a more traditional style, immediately switched to bluegrass; Flatt and Scruggs left Monroe to form their own group, which achieved great success from the mid-1950s through the late '60s. These three groups would become the templates for dozens more.

The rise of rock 'n' roll

In 1954, a young Memphis-born singer entered a tiny recording studio to cut his first disc under the watchful eye of the studio's owner and engineer, Sam Phillips. Memphis was home to two vibrant musical communities: a "country" one in which white musicians performed primarily for a white audience and a "blues" scene catering to African Americans. Despite this de facto segregation, radio crossed racial lines, so that many white listeners were furtively listening to and enjoying blues music. Phillips had begun his career in radio before opening his small Sun record label; with a racially open policy, Phillips had already recorded both black and white artists in his one-room studio. He also ran a recording service where, for a fee, musicians could cut personal records.

A recent high school graduate came by to make a disc for his mother. Whether it was Phillips himself or his secretary who was struck by his talents, eventually he was called back to make a record for Phillips's Sun label. The artist was named Elvis Presley; Phillips encouraged him to record a "cover" of a previous R&B hit, Blind Boy Crudup's "That's Alright Mama." Employing two local band musicians to accompany the young singer, it took Phillips several hours to capture the sound he was hoping to achieve. When asked for a second song they could use for the record's flip side, Elvis began fooling around with a recent country hit, Bill Monroe's "Blue Moon of Kentucky." Just as during 1927's "big bang" sessions Ralph Peer recorded both a black-influenced act (Jimmie Rodgers) and a more white, traditional one (the Carter Family), Elvis's first record wed black and white influences—although both were modernized in a fresh, rhythmic performance that heralded a revolution in popular music: the rise of rock 'n' roll.

On the heels of his first record, Elvis hit the road, appearing mostly as a second or third act on an all-country bill. His biggest early break came on October 6, 1954, when he was hired as a regular on the *Louisiana Hayride*. Elvis remained at the *Hayride* for eighteen months; when he left the station in 1956 and signed with RCA as a teen pop star, the program began its long decline.

Elvis became one of pop's most successful artists—but the shadow of his success cast an initial pall over country music, which suddenly sounded old-fashioned to younger audiences. Major country acts scrambled for literally years to try to regain their popularity.

One response among country performers was to adapt elements of Elvis's style—particularly its strong backbeat and swinging accompaniments—along with Western swing and other more progressive country elements to create a new style nicknamed "rockabilly." Another Sun artist helped originate this style, singer and guitarist Carl Lee Perkins. Born to a poor farming family in Tiptonville, Tennessee (about 125 miles north of Memphis), Perkins was exposed to music from an early age. His father was an avid fan of the *Grand Ole Opry*, and it was one of the few radio shows he would allow to be played in the family home. A second important influence was a black sharecropper who played guitar in a fingerpicking blues style.

The family moved after World War II, when Carl's father joined his brothers working in a cotton mill. They settled in their first home with electricity, and soon Carl was practicing on a second-hand electric guitar. In the early 1950s, Carl talked his brothers into forming a country trio, and they began performing in local honky-tonks. After a while, it became clear to Carl that the group would need drums if they were to provide a danceable beat for their customers. His brother Clayton brought on board schoolmate W. S. "Fluke" Holland, who had a keen appreciation for R&B music as well as country. Carl, meanwhile, was moving the music in an uptempo direction to suit dancing, thus setting the foundation for rockabilly.

In 1954, Perkins heard Elvis Presley's recording of "Blue Moon of Kentucky" and realized that someone else was experimenting with uptempo country music. He took his brothers to Memphis in search of Sun Records, where he met owner Sam Phillips. After recording a few country numbers, Perkins performed "Gone, Gone, Gone," which featured a rocking beat along with scat vocals, followed in late 1955 by "Blue Suede Shoes" and "Honey Don't." "Blue Suede Shoes" established Perkins's reputation, making him an instant star. However, Perkins's new success was short-lived. While on the road to New York to perform on a TV show in early 1956, his manager fell asleep at the wheel, and all three Perkins brothers were injured. Perkins struggled to re-establish himself, first as a rock artist and later as a country performer, but his unique guitar playing and songwriting had already made a lasting mark. The Beatles' George Harrison was just one influential leader in the British rock invasion who attested to Perkins's considerable impact on his music.

There were also female rockabilly stars, most notably Wanda Jackson. Jackson was born in rural Oklahoma, although the family soon relocated to Bakersfield, California—a town that attracted many fellow Okies displaced by the Dust Bowl during the 1930s. She met Hank Thompson there, who brought her to Capitol Records—who told her that "girls don't sell records." Nonetheless, she ultimately recorded for the label, releasing a string of rockabilly-flavored singles, many with then-session guitarist Buck Owens. Most were only minor, local hits at the time, but many, such as "Hot Dog! That Made Him Mad," "Fujiyama Mama," and "Honey Bop," are now considered rockabilly classics. Wanda's tough-girl image—she appeared in fringed cowgirl jackets and high heels, eschewing the gingham dresses and demure appearance of singers like Kitty Wells—also brought her great notoriety.

Return to roots: The folk balladeers

When the country and western charts were first established, another popular style—urban "folk" music—was included within this general category. Groups like the New York–based Weavers were (briefly) successful on the pop charts in the late 1940s and early '50s, although their progressive politics came back to haunt them. When senator Joe McCarthy began his attack on so-called communists, many folk performers disappeared from the radio and record. However, in the late '50s, a new generation of performers—unstained by any earlier political affiliations—were able to bring back "folk" styles to the charts. Most notably, the college-educated members of the Kingston Trio hit the charts with their hit "Tom Dooley" in 1958—originally recorded by the country duo Grayson and Whitter in 1929.

The craze for folk-themed songs did not go unnoticed by country performers who were still trying to recover from the rise of Elvis Presley. Honky-tonk singer Johnny Horton had befriended Hank Williams when both were appearing on the *Louisiana Hayride*. After many missed opportunities, he had a hit in 1956 with "Honky Tonk Man," but then watched his fame slip away once again. But, he made a comeback with the folk-ballad-influenced song and his first country number-one hit, 1958's "When It's Springtime in Alaska." The ever-popular "Battle of New Orleans" followed that same year. The song was written by Arkansas-born songwriter Jimmy Driftwood, who recorded it for RCA on the oddly named album *Newly Discovered Early American Folk Songs*—odd because, in fact, the songs on this record were entirely new and simply written in the style of "early folk songs." The "Battle of New Orleans" told the story of the final, decisive battle of the War of 1812 between the British and the Americans, which took place outside of New Orleans in 1814. It was set to the traditional fiddle tune, "The Eighth of January." Horton's version topped the charts for ten weeks and reached gold (that is, million-selling) status. This led RCA to release Driftwood's version that June, which was a top-twenty-five country hit. Horton followed with a slew of other hits in the folk ballad style, including 1959's "Johnny Reb" and 1960's "Sink the Bismarck" and "North to Alaska."

Another artist who would try on various styles was singer Marty Robbins. Raised in the small town of Glendale, Arizona, Martin

David Robinson enlisted in the Navy in 1944 and was stationed in the Pacific when he began to write and perform original songs. On his return after the war, Robbins drifted from job to job, while performing locally in clubs and bars at night. He took the name "Marty Robbins" because it sounded a little more Western than his real name.

By the early '50s, Marty was performing on a local radio station, KPHO, hosting his own *Western Caravan* show. Little Jimmy Dickens was a guest on the show and was so impressed that he recommended that his record label sign Robbins. In 1953, Robbins joined the *Grand Ole Opry*, where he remained a member for twenty-nine years, until his death. Two months after his first *Opry* appearance, Robbins scored his first top-ten country hit, "I'll Go on Alone." But for the next two years, Robbins struggled to place his songs on the country charts. His next big break came in 1956 with "Singing the Blues," followed a year later by "Knee Deep in the Blues," "The Story of My Life," and "A White Sport Coat (and a Pink Carnation)." These rockabilly-flavored songs, featuring Marty's peppy, smooth vocals, not only scored big on the country charts, but also helped him break through into the pop charts. He continued in this pop-influenced vein through the '50s, turning out 1958's "She Was Only Seventeen" and "Stairway of Love."

Robbins turned to cowboy-flavored material with his appearance in the 1958 film *Buffalo Gun*. He recorded his classic album of Western story songs, *Gunfighter Ballads and Trail Songs*, a year later, producing several hits, most notably "El Paso," a song that would become closely associated with him. It topped both the country and pop charts and won the first Grammy Award ever given to a country song. Robbins followed it with more folk-flavored numbers, including "Big Iron" and "Battle of the Alamo."

Rockabilly and folk-flavored country were both attempts by country artists to regain their popularity in the wake of the rise of rock 'n' roll. But by far the most far-reaching and controversial (to traditional country fans) response was being developed by key producers who felt that country needed to modernize its sound in order to appeal to a new generation of listeners. This music—which would come to be called "countrypolitan" or the "Nashville sound"—would dominate the country charts through most of the next decade.

5

"Make the world go away": Countrypolitan sounds, 1957–1964

The rise of rock 'n' roll shook Nashville, as it did the rest of the popular music world. While some performers tried to wed country sounds with a rock beat in a new style called "rockabilly," Nashville's music industry itself turned to popular stylings to reach a new audience. Leading producers like Owen Bradley, Chet Atkins, and Billy Sherrill wed light jazz and pop sounds to create a new style that came to be known as the "Nashville sound." Gone were fiddles and banjos; in their place were string sections and vocal choirs. Notable performers in this new style include Eddy Arnold (who had previously performed in a Western-folk style), Patsy Cline (in her later hits), George Jones (in his post-honky-tonk recordings), and Tammy Wynette. The Nashville sound matured in the late '60s into "countrypolitan," blending elements of orchestral pop, adult contemporary, and light rock into a winning formula for country stars.

Escaping the hayloft: A new generation comes to Nashville

In the mid-'50s, some younger, Nashville-based musicians were embarrassed by the "old-fashioned" musical styles and hillbilly routines employed by older acts. They thought the clichéd image of the fiddle-sawing, banjo-banging backwoodsman was limiting country music's reach; many were more interested in playing jazz than country, which they felt was a more sophisticated musical style. A leader of this movement was Chet Atkins, whose elder brother was a talented jazz guitarist and who loved the chamber-style jazz that was popular in the '50s. An informal group of musicians began jamming with Atkins in Nashville's clubs, including pianist Floyd Cramer, master saxophonist Boots Randolph, and drummer Buddy Harman.

Atkins came from a musical family; his grandfather was a well-known fiddler, and his father taught music, tuned pianos, and worked as a revivalist preacher. His parents separated when he was young, and Chet got his first guitar from his stepfather when he was about nine years old. At age seventeen, Atkins found radio work, eventually working as staff guitarist for a station out of Knoxville, Tennessee. Beginning in the mid-'40s, Atkins also worked as an accompanist for various country acts (including the Carter Family and country comedians Homer and Jethro) on radio and on the road. He began recording as a soloist in the late '40s.

Atkins continued recording as a solo guitarist from the late '40s through the early '50s, showing a knack for combining country swing, blues, and jazz influences in his electric guitar–focused instrumentals. They set new standards for performance, including 1947's "Canned Heat," 1949's "Galloping on the Guitar," and his best-known composition, 1953's "Country Gentleman." He also was hired by the Gretsch guitar company, which produced several signature guitars under his name, including the hollow-bodied, electric Country Gentleman model. In 1957, RCA Victor hired Atkins to be their A&R manager. Naturally, he hired many of his friends from the local scene for the sessions he produced; these included everyone from rocker Elvis Presley to mainstream country acts. He brought a new level of pop sophistication to these sessions, filling out the instrumental accompaniments with the smooth vocal accompaniments of the Jordanaires and the Anita

Kerr Singers, again to soften the rough edges of country recordings.

Among the most prominent sidemen of this period was pianist Floyd Cramer, who can be heard on countless country sessions from the mid-'50s through the early '70s. Cramer began taking piano lessons at age five, and he first played professionally for local dances while still in high school. He joined the *Louisiana Hayride* radio program as a staff accompanist after graduating from high school in 1951. He worked briefly for the Abbott label and then teamed up with Chet Atkins as house pianist at RCA, recording behind a young Elvis Presley, Jim Reeves, and countless others. Influenced by the picking of Mother Maybelle Carter and the piano playing of Don Robertson, he developed his characteristic "slip note" style of playing, in which he imitates the sliding from note to note that is possible on guitar or fiddle by hitting one note and almost immediately sliding his finger onto the next key. Like Atkins, Cramer was influenced by the light jazz of '50s acts like Nat King Cole.

In a similar move, producer Owen Bradley at Decca focused throughout the '50s on updating country music to make it more popular. Bradley was born in Westmoreland, Tennessee, northeast of Nashville, and began his career as a piano and guitar player in various pop pickup bands in and around Nashville after World War II. In 1947, he was selected to be the orchestra leader for radio station WSM, home of the *Grand Ole Opry*. That same year, he was hired to produce recordings for Decca Records, which wanted to establish a presence in country music. In 1954, along with his brother, guitarist Harold Bradley, Owen opened a small recording studio in an abandoned Quonset hut on his family's property. This was the first working studio on what would become Nashville's "Music Row." Employing his brother as a guitarist, along with many of the same musicians who worked for Atkins, Bradley helped solidify the Nashville sound as the predominant approach to country recording.

"Make the world go away"

Although Bradley recorded everything from Bill Monroe's bluegrass to Ernest Tubb's original honky-tonk sessions, he is most famous for his late '50s and early '60s recordings of crossover artists like Brenda Lee and Patsy Cline. Born Virginia Patterson Hensley in Winchester, Virginia, Cline won an amateur talent contest as a tap dancer when she was four and began singing soon after. Winning an audition with Wally Fowler of the *Grand Ole Opry* when she was sixteen, young Cline so impressed him that he invited her to Nashville; however, she was unable to obtain a recording contract and eventually returned to her hometown. She performed throughout her high school years, eventually signing with the local Four Star label in 1956. Originally, the label promoted her as a modern cowgirl, dressing her in fringed jackets and having her cut songs in the honky-tonk mold. Her first hit came in 1957 with "Walkin' after Midnight," which is often interpreted as the story of a woman abandoned by her man, who is perhaps out honky-tonking.

The song's success led to a contract with Decca Records, where Cline worked with Owen Bradley from 1957 to 1960, gaining moderate success on the country charts. Over these years, Bradley transformed Cline into the kind of dreamy, pop chanteuse that could appeal to a broad audience. Cline hated the more pop-oriented material, but her cool, gliding vocals became the model for hundreds of country singers to come, who gave up the old Mountain Dew for the bubbly champagne of mainstream pop. It wasn't until 1961's "Crazy" (written by Willie Nelson), followed by "I Fall to Pieces," that her characteristic, sad-and-lonesome vocal sound fell into place. A two-year hit-making span followed, including "Leavin' on Your Mind" and the posthumously released "Sweet Dreams." Decca promoted her as a mainstream pop chanteuse, dressing her in evening gowns and adding strings and vocal choruses to her records. Cline's death in an airplane accident on March 5, 1963, helped solidify her place in the country music pantheon.

8. **Patsy Cline collaborated with popular country singer Ferlin Huskey in the late 1950s. She had already made the transition from cowgirl fringe to lounge-singer glitz.**

Another convert to the Nashville sound was Brenda Lee (b. Brenda Mae Tarpley). She performed on country radio as early as age seven in and around Atlanta, Georgia. When she was eleven, Decca signed her to a contract, and she had her first hit with "Dynamite" a year later, a rockabilly song that gave her her nickname, "Little Miss Dyn-a-mite." Lee continued to record in the rockabilly mold through the early '60s, including the novelty Christmas classic, "Rockin' around the Christmas Tree." In the early '60s, Lee paired with producer Owen Bradley, who directed her transition to the Nashville sound. Together, the duo produced a string of classic country weepers, including 1960's "I'm Sorry," "Dum Dum," and "Fool No. 1" from 1961, "All Alone Am I" and "Break It to Me Gently" from 1962, and 1963's "Losing You."

Nashville had become a professional music-making center by the early '60s. The local session musicians prided themselves on their ability to accompany anybody. Although some developed a distinctive style (such as Cramer's "slip-note" piano playing), the emphasis was on a homogenized, one-sound-fits-all style of playing that inevitably took the character out of the music. This, combined with the advent of large music publishing houses (beginning with Acuff–Rose), led Nashville to become a Tin Pan Alley of the South. Unlike folk and rock, where the trend was toward songwriters performing their own material (and becoming stars), in country the music was still dominated by "professionals" who carefully molded the music to fit its audience.

Riding the Nashville sound to stardom

For many country performers who had initially found success in the late '40s and early '50s—only to watch their careers seemingly disappear overnight in the wake of rock 'n' roll—the Nashville sound helped them regain their place on the country charts. Among the first to ride this new style to success was singer Eddy Arnold. The son of an old-time fiddler father and guitar-playing mother, Arnold took up the guitar at age ten, abandoning his schooling soon after to help during the Depression years on his family's farm. After performing at local dances, Arnold was hired to perform on local radio, which in turn led to additional jobs in Memphis and St. Louis. Arnold enjoyed his first success as a performer when he was hired in the early '40s to sing with Pee Wee King's Golden West Cowboys, a popular group on the *Grand Ole Opry*. Given his early experiences on the farm, Arnold earned the nickname "the Tennessee Ploughboy."

In 1944, Arnold signed as a solo act with RCA and had his first string of hits with honky-tonk and cowboy numbers between the late '40s and early '50s, including 1948's sentimental "Bouquet of Roses," 1951's "I Wanna Play House with You," and 1955's Western epic, "Cattle Call." In the mid-'50s, Arnold hosted his own syndicated TV program; he was also invited as a guest on many of the popular variety programs catering to a general audience. However, for ten years he fell off the country charts, not returning until the mid-'60s with a string of pop-flavored hits. On records like "Make the World Go Away" (also a top-ten pop hit), "Lonely Again," and "Turn the World Around," Arnold successfully wed blue-and-lonesome subject matter with mainstream appeal. Featuring pianist Floyd Cramer and the Anita Kerr Singers, these recordings launched Arnold as a pop vocalist. He put aside his country garb for a classy tux.

Another '50s-era star who "crossed over" to pop success in the '60s was singer Jim Reeves. Reeves showed an early interest in music and was given a guitar by a construction worker friend of the family when he was five years old. He made his first radio broadcast at age nine in Shreveport. After World War II, Jim worked as a radio announcer, thanks to his baritone voice, which carried well over the air. In 1949, he made a few recordings for a small, Houston-based label, and by 1951 or 1952 he was announcing for the *Louisiana Hayride*. He was heard performing on the *Hayride* by Fabor Robison of Abbott Records, who immediately signed him.

Reeves's first country hit was 1953's "Mexican Joe." In 1955, he moved to the *Grand Ole Opry* and signed with RCA, where he quickly produced the hit "Yonder Comes a Sucker." In 1957, he scored his first crossover hit on the pop charts with "Four Walls," leading to many TV appearances. From 1960 to his untimely death on July 31, 1964, in an airplane crash, Reeves was rarely off the charts, beginning with "I'm Getting Better" from 1960, through 1962's "Adios Amigo" and 1963's "Is This Me?," to his last single released while he was still alive, "Welcome to My World."

After his death, Reeve's wife arranged for his unissued material to be released, and his popularity grew from the first posthumous single, 1964's "I Guess I'm Crazy."

Some rockabilly stars also found renewed success embracing the Nashville sound, most prominently Charlie Rich and Conway Twitty. Rich was greatly influenced by jazz and blues as a young musician. Unlike many other country performers, he studied music in college. He joined the Air Force and was stationed in Oklahoma, where he formed his first semiprofessional combo. After leaving the service, Rich returned to West Memphis, Arkansas, to help his father work his cotton farm. Rich crossed the river to Memphis to work as a session pianist for Sun Records, appearing on many of its late '50s recordings, and scored his first solo hit with 1959's "Lonely Weekends."

Rich struggled in the first half of the 1960s to find his sound, moving from the boogie-woogie-influenced "Big Boss Man" of 1963 to the country novelty of "Mohair Sam." In 1968, he was signed to major label Epic Records and producer Billy Sherrill, a younger executive who would play a role in transforming the Nashville sound into countrypolitan music. It took five years for Rich and Sherrill to hit a winning formula, but they hit it big from 1973 to 1975 with songs like "Behind Closed Doors," "The Most Beautiful Girl in the World," "A Very Special Love Song," and "Every Time You Touch Me." Rich continued to have hits through 1979's "I'll Wake You Up When I Get Home," but after that his days of chart-topping success were over. Rich died from a blood clot in the lung at the age of sixty-two.

Conway Twitty was born Harold Jenkins in the small Mississippi riverfront town of Friars Point. His father gave him his first rudimentary guitar lessons; young Jenkins had his own country band performing on the radio by the time he was ten years old. After serving in the Army in the mid-'50s, Jenkins heard the first Elvis recordings and, inspired by Elvis's success, he adopted the new rockabilly sound. He decided that, if he was going to be a rock star, he needed a rock star's name. Looking on a map, he hit on the names of two local towns: Twitty, Texas, and Conway, Arkansas. He called his band the Twitty Birds. (Later, when he achieved success as a country star, he made his home into a theme park, aptly called Twitty City.)

Twitty's first big hit came in 1958 with "It's Only Make Believe," which he cowrote, a million-seller on the pop chart. A number of rockabilly and teen pop singles followed, including 1960's hit "Lonely Blue Boy." His success won him the attention of Hollywood and, like Elvis, he appeared in a number of forgettable low-budget films performing his music, including the memorably titled *Sex Kittens Go to College* and *Platinum High*. But, after the Beatles broke through onto the charts in 1964, Conway's pop career fizzled and he relocated to Nashville, where he became a major star. His first big country hit came in 1970 with "Hello Darlin'," which was followed by several more charting singles throughout the decade. Most of his best songs were on the subjects of lovin', leavin', and loneliness—classic country concerns—from the humorous ("Tight Fittin' Jeans") to the sentimental ("After All the Good Is Gone"). The production values were pure Nashville sound, with silky accompaniments and smooth backup vocals.

At the same time, he began a successful collaboration with singer Loretta Lynn. Their duets included sexually suggestive numbers that initially upset mainstream country deejays. Their first hit, 1971's "After the Fire Is Gone," reflected a typical Twitty concern: a relationship on the skids. Other numbers celebrated regional identity ("Louisiana Woman, Mississippi Man") and down-home humor ("You're the Reason Our Kids Are Ugly").

Transcending the Nashville sound: Loretta Lynn and Dolly Parton

Two female singer–songwriters who achieved fame during the Nashville sound years transcended many of its limitations to create truly original and unique recordings: Loretta Lynn and Dolly Parton. One of country music's pioneering female performers and songwriters, Loretta Lynn has a classic country voice that is perfectly suited to her to-the-point lyrics reflecting a uniquely female outlook. Perhaps the only country singer who has taken on a wide variety of issues, from birth control to the Vietnam War to spousal abuse, Lynn has made an important contribution to widening the subject matter and audience for country music.

Loretta Webb was born in a small coal-mining community, Butcher Hollow, Kentucky. When she was thirteen, she married Oliver "Mooney" Lynn, who later became her manager. The couple relocated to Washington State, where Lynn raised four children while she began performing her own material. Her first single, "I'm a Honky Tonk Girl," released in 1960 on the tiny Zero label, was in the classic barroom mold. This brought her to the attention of Owen Bradley, the legendary producer who had worked with Patsy Cline.

Lynn's recordings from the early 1960s showed the influence of Kitty Wells in their brash lyrics centered on themes of lovin' and losin'. Soon, however, her vocal style softened, while her original material turned to unusual (for the time) topics, including "Don't Come Home a-Drinkin' (with Lovin' on Your Mind)," "You Ain't Woman Enough (to Take My Man)," and "The Pill," a song in support of birth control. All of the songs were written from a woman's point of view, and their messages were unusually liberated for the '60s and early '70s. This heavy dose of reality pointed the direction for many of the more progressive country songwriters of the '70s and '80s. Lynn's autobiographical song "Coal Miner's Daughter," from 1970, perfectly expressed the pride and anguish of growing up dirt poor in the mountains. Her autobiography of the same name, published in 1976, was instrumental not only in cementing her image as a "true country woman," but in reasserting country music's roots at a time when many acts were trying to cross over onto the pop and rock charts. It in turn inspired a major film starring Sissy Spacek that only increased her fame.

In 1988, Lynn was elected to the Country Music Hall of Fame. From 1990 to 1996, she withdrew from performing in order to nurse her ailing husband, who finally succumbed to diabetes in August 1996. She returned to performing on a limited basis thereafter, although she has also suffered from time to time with health problems of her own. In 2003, she was awarded a Kennedy Center Honor, and the following year she issued her first new album of original material in many years, working with alt-rocker Jack White of the White Stripes, which established her as a star among a new generation of listeners.

The fourth of twelve children, Dolly Rebecca Parton was born in rural Locust Ridge, Tennessee. Parton's first recordings were made in 1959 when she was still a teen; in 1964, she traveled to Nashville and scored her first hit with "Dumb Blonde" in 1967. That same year, she joined forces with country legend Porter Wagoner, a savvy businessman who ran a large country revue. He recorded a string of duets with the younger singer, beginning with a cover of Tom Paxton's "Last Thing on My Mind," which helped launch her career.

Dolly's solo recordings from RCA in the late '60s and early '70s established her as a sensitive singer–songwriter who could reflect on her own rural heritage. In songs like 1971's "Coat of Many Colors," she honored the memory of her mother, who made her a patchwork coat out of fabric remnants. Her biggest hit came in 1973 with "Jolene," which addressed a husband-stealing woman in a forthright and strong way, thus reversing a classic honky-tonk theme. In 1974, Parton permanently split from Wagoner and scored a number-one country hit with "I Will Always Love You" (later a number-one hit for pop singer Whitney Houston in 1992–1993). In the later '70s, Parton crossed over to the pop charts, beginning with the bouncy 1977 hit, "Here You Come Again," followed by the light pop of 1980's "9 to 5," the theme song of the movie that briefly launched Parton's acting career. This success led to a decade of minor and major film roles, plus continued recordings in a pop-country vein. Parton also showed savvy as a businesswoman, opening her own theme park, Dollywood, to celebrate Tennessee mountain crafts and culture.

The birth of countrypolitan

The pop leanings of the successful purveyors of the Nashville sound led to an even more radical adoption of mainstream pop music that became known as "countrypolitan." A play on words combining "country" and "cosmopolitan," this label was applied to the music that came out of Nashville from the late '60s through the new country revolution of the mid-1980s. Producers and performers alike wanted to compete head-to-head with middle-of-the-road pop music in order to cross over to the more lucrative "adult contemporary" market. With countrypolitan music, Nashville's professional music establishment turned to pop styles and "countrified" them.

The movement began with soft pop singers who tried to move a little more toward a rock sound. Lynn Anderson's upbeat 1970 hit "(I Never Promised You a) Rose Garden" is one of the first examples of a pop-inflected song that came out of the country charts. Anderson was the daughter of honky-tonk songwriter Liz Anderson, who was best known for the hits she penned for Merle Haggard, including "Lonesome Fugitive" and "My Friends Are Gonna Be Strangers." Lynn Anderson was born in Grand Forks, North Dakota, and raised in California. She first found success on the local horse-show circuit while also working as a singer on *The Lawrence Welk Show*. In 1968, she moved to Nashville and, a year later, had a number-three country hit with "That's a No No." She married producer–songwriter R. Glenn Sutton, who produced her biggest hit in 1970, "(I Never Promised You a) Rose Garden," the title song of a successful film. The poppy, upbeat song featured a light rock accompaniment and not only topped the country charts but reached number three on the pop charts, making it a highly unusual crossover hit. Anderson would produce many more country hits through the '70s, including 1973's "Top of the World," which reached number two on the country charts and number one—in a cover by the Carpenters—on the pop charts.

An even bigger splash was made by Crystal Gayle, whose 1978 hit "Don't It Make My Brown Eyes Blue," with its tinkling piano and oh-so-pleasant vocal, is perhaps the definitive countrypolitan recording. The youngest sister of country star Loretta Lynn, Brenda Gail Webb was born in Paintsville, Kentucky. She began her career when she was sixteen, singing backup vocals for her sister and Conway Twitty. Lynn gave her her stage name, perhaps inspired by the country chain of Krystal hamburger stands. Gayle made her first solo recordings at age nineteen with her sister's country weeper, "I Cried (The Blue Right out of My Eyes)," but did not crack the country charts again for five years.

Resisting the efforts of Nashville to mold her into a younger Loretta Lynn, Gayle finally hooked up with producer Allen Reynolds, who supplied her 1975 hit "Wrong Road Again." Three years later, she scored a major pop crossover hit with "Don't It Make My Brown Eyes Blue," her best-known recording. She had a few more pop successes in the late '70s.

A key producer in the countrypolitan style was Billy Sherrill, who guided the successful careers of Tammy Wynette and George Jones, among many others. Sherrill got his start working for Sam Phillips's Sun Records in the early '60s, producing country and rock artists. He moved to Epic Records, a division of Columbia, where he brought his interest in jazz, mainstream pop, and light rock to his country producing. He became the "go-to" producer for countrypolitan stars beginning with his work with Wynette.

"Make the world go away"

Virginia Wynette Pugh was born near Tupelo, Mississippi, and showed early musical talents, playing several instruments as well as singing. She moved to Birmingham, Alabama, during her teen years and was married for the first time at age seventeen. Wynette worked as a beautician during the day and club singer at night to support her three children. She went to Nashville in the mid-'60s in search of a career, auditioning for several labels while working as a singer and song plugger. Producer Billy Sherrill recognized her potential and signed her to Epic, where she had an immediate hit with 1966's "Apartment Number 9," followed by the racy (for the time) "Your Good Girl's Gonna Go Bad." Wynette's tough-girl image was underscored in a series of hits, including "I Don't Wanna Play House" from 1967 and "D-I-V-O-R-C-E" from 1968. The same year brought "Stand by Your Man," perhaps Wynette's most famous recording and one that continues to inspire controversy due to its message that a woman must support her husband—no matter what. She had more hits in 1969: "Singing My Song" and "The Ways to Love a Man."

In 1968, Wynette began a stormy, seven-year marriage to the hard-living country star George Jones. The duo often recorded together, including an album of duets from 1972 (with a hit in 1973 with "We're Gonna Hold On") and again in 1976, hitting it big with "Golden Ring" and "Near You" (even though they had divorced in 1975); they teamed up again in 1980, scoring a hit with "Two-Story House." Meanwhile, Tammy continued to record as a solo artist through the '70s, scoring major hits through the middle of the decade, including 1972's "Bedtime Story" and "My Man (Understands)" (which clones the sentiments of "Stand by Your Man"), 1974's "Another Lonely Song," and her last solo, number-one, country hit, "You and Me" from 1976. Many of these songs were cowritten by producer Sherrill and were carefully crafted to fit Wynette's image.

George Jones also scored under Sherrill's guidance as a solo artist. Born in Saratoga, in southeast Texas, he began performing honky-tonk material after his discharge from the Marines in the early '50s. In 1954, he teamed up with manager/record producer Harold "Pappy" Daily. Jones's early records showed the influence of Hank Williams, although he also briefly jumped on the rockabilly bandwagon, recording under the name "Thumper Jones." Jones's first big country hits came in the early '60s with songs drenched in honky-tonk heartache, including 1962's "She Thinks I Still Care" and 1964's "The Race Is On." Hearing Wynette's hits in 1966, he was immediately attracted to the singer.

Jones married Tammy Wynette in 1969 and moved to her label, Epic, in 1971, where he began working with producer Billy Sherrill as well. Besides their hits as a duo, Jones found success under Sherrill's guidance, including 1974's "The Grand Tour" and "The Door," both heavily produced with strings and vocal choruses that nonetheless could not obscure Jones's honky-tonk soul. Sherrill oversaw Jones's biggest hit, 1980's "He Stopped Loving Her Today," a song that Jones was initially hesitant to record, telling his producer "Nobody'll buy that morbid son of a bitch." Nonetheless, it was the biggest song of his career.

Both Jones and Wynette would see their careers decline due to changing musical tastes and personal struggles—Jones with his alcoholism and drug abuse and Wynette with health issues. Jones saw a career revival during the "new country" years of the '80s, and the duo even managed to record a final duet together in 1995. Wynette passed away three years later, while Jones enjoyed a brief career resurgence thanks to the rise of new country in the mid-'90s, passing away in 2013.

Kenny Rogers was the ultimate countrypolitan star. Coming from a folk-pop background, Rogers had a husky voice, sexy good looks, and a repertoire of soft pop ballads that appealed to a mainstream audience. In the late '60s, he formed the folk-tinged pop vocal group the First Edition, scoring a major pop hit with 1967's "Just

Dropped in (to See What Condition My Condition Was In)."
Other hits, in a more country vein, followed, including "Ruby
(Don't Take Your Love to Town)." The group remained together
under Rogers's leadership until 1975, when he embarked on a
solo career.

The late '70s were golden years for Rogers, beginning in 1977 with
his monster hit "Lucille," establishing him as a star on both
country and pop charts. He followed it with a hit 1978 duet with
Dottie West on "Every Time Two Fools Collide," solidifying his
position as a country music star. Later that same year, he scored
on his own with "The Gambler," which became his best-loved
country-flavored song (and also inspired a made-for-TV movie
two years later). By the late '70s, his dress style indicated a basic
change in the country audience; no Nudie suits or ten-gallon hats
for this cowboy, but rather, ready-to-wear disco clothes, complete
with unbuttoned shirts, chains, and bell bottoms. Rogers reached
out to the pop audience by recording duets with pop-rocker Kim
Carnes on "Don't Fall in Love with a Dreamer" in 1980 and with
R&B balladeer Lionel Richie on the ballad "Lady."

While the countrypolitan movement was in full flower, stirrings of
revolt could be felt among some country performers. Even during
its period of greatest success, hard-core country music was still
being recorded in places beyond Nashville's orbit, particularly in
Bakersfield, California. Meanwhile, in the later '60s, a group of
so-called outlaws turned their backs on Nashville, heading to
places like Austin, Texas, to create a new music by focusing on
older country styles. And a bluegrass revival was sweeping
through the folk community; many of these younger pickers
would become the new country stars of the '80s and '90s.

6

"Mama tried": Country alternatives, 1965–1980

While the Nashville sound dominated much of country radio in the '60s and countrypolitan turbocharged its pop leanings in the '70s, there were still other styles of country music that would ultimately help bring a revival of "traditional" country sounds back to the charts. Out in Bakersfield, California, in the 1960s—where many displaced southwesterners settled following the harrowing dust storms of the 1930s—a new amalgam of rockabilly, honky-tonk, and Western swing was being developed by artists like Merle Haggard and Buck Owens. Back in Nashville, some artists, like Willie Nelson, found themselves uncomfortably shoe-horned by the major labels into recording with vocal choruses, strings, and light pop accompaniments. Nelson and his cohorts would eventually rebel against these limitations, resulting in the "outlaw country" movement of the late '60s and early '70s. The outlaws represented a return to country's roots in honky-tonk and Western swing stylings, which were then wed with the influence of the '60s singer–songwriters and country rock. Nelson, Waylon Jennings, Kris Kristofferson, and Jessi Colter—among others—created a new style and sound that had crossover appeal to a younger audience.

Other artists during the period didn't seem to fit into any stylistic mold—or rather, they formed their own unique sounds, which set them apart from all others. A key performer who shaped his own career in unusual ways was Johnny Cash, whose stripped-down recordings melded folk, rockabilly, blues, and country into a singular, immediately recognizable mix. And a younger generation of performers—raised on folk, bluegrass, and pop-rock music—began to discover the allure of country music, forming new styles that would become known as country rock and progressive bluegrass.

Bakersfield and Southern California country

About a hundred miles north of Los Angeles lies the oil-boom town of Bakersfield. From the mid-'30s through the '40s, many displaced southwesterners, particularly from Oklahoma, came to the town in search of work. The oil industry provided good jobs that paid well, and soon a local club scene was thriving to cater to the tastes of the displaced Okies. Bakersfield was also home to a major military base, with soldiers stationed there from around the country who were hungry for entertainment. Local dance halls soon sprang up, attracting musicians seeking work who were able to perform on a circuit that went through the area and reached the outskirts of Los Angeles and as far north as Sacramento. Small labels in the area capitalized on this new sound, quickly signing contracts with local acts. In 1951, a new television show, *Town Hall Party*, began broadcasting; it featured Western swing players like Bob Wills and eventually many local bands as well.

One of the first stars to break out of the Western mold from the area was Tommy Collins, who featured a stripped-down, honky-tonk sound in his band and recordings, thanks to lead guitarist Buck Owens. Owens was soon a star on his own, leading a hot country combo from the late '50s through the '60s, featuring lead guitar parts and vocal harmonies by Don Rich, who played the newly introduced Fender Telecaster guitar, as well as steel guitarist Tom Brumley.

Born Alvis Edgar Owens Jr. in Sherman, Texas, Buck was the son of a sharecropper. Early in his life, the family moved to Arizona in search of a better standard of living, but to little avail, and Buck had to leave school after the ninth grade to help support his family. Already a talented musician who played both mandolin and guitar, he was performing on local radio out of Mesa when he was just sixteen; he met future wife, Bonnie Campbell Owens, there and married her a year later. Bonnie would have a minor career of her own as a country singer and would later marry Merle Haggard.

In 1951, Buck relocated to Bakersfield, where he formed his first band, while also working as a guitarist on numerous country and pop-rock sessions. Owens also recorded some rockabilly tunes under the name "Corky Jones." After working with Tommy Collins for a few years, Owens formed his own band, the Buckaroos, in the late '50s, signing to Capitol as a solo performer.

Owens's first regional hits were "Second Fiddle," followed by "Under Your Spell Again" from 1959, "Excuse Me, I Think I've Got a Heartache" from a year later, and 1961's "Fooling Around." From the first, Owens established himself as a purveyor of upbeat, honky-tonk-flavored material. Owens charted consistently throughout the '60s, with wonderful hits such as 1963's "Act Naturally," "I've Got a Tiger by the Tail" and "Buckaroo" from 1965, "Waitin' in Your Welfare Line" from a year later, and 1969's "Tall Dark Stranger." He also made some fine duet recordings in the early '60s with Western swing-turned-bluegrass vocalist Rose Maddox.

In 1969, Owens was hired to cohost a new country music TV show called *Hee Haw*. The show's combination of cornball humor and teary-eyed country music dated back to the minstrel and tent shows that had toured the South beginning in the mid-nineteenth century; the quick editing from joke to joke was borrowed from a popular TV series of the day, *Laugh-In*. The success of the show made Buck one of the most instantly identifiable of all country stars. He made several "comebacks" in later decades, particularly when new stars like Dwight Yoakam revived the Bakersfield sound.

A Bakersfield native named Merle Haggard furthered the roots-oriented style, performing songs about his real-life experiences. Haggard was born in Bakersfield, but like so many of their neighbors, Haggard's parents were displaced Oklahoma farmers who were driven off their land by the ravaging dust storms of the mid-'30s. They found living conditions tough in California and jobs few; the family was living in a converted boxcar when Haggard was born. They fared better after Merle's father got a job with the Santa Fe Railroad, but this brief period of prosperity ended with his premature death when Merle was nine.

Haggard attributes his troubled teenage years to his father's passing. He became difficult and unruly, constantly running away from home. He ended up serving time in reform school, and then, when he reached age seventeen, he served ninety days in prison for stealing. However, when he was released he was soon in trouble, and he was arrested again after a botched attempt at robbing a local restaurant. Haggard spent the next two and a half years in prison. While there, he heard Johnny Cash perform, which renewed his interest in country music and his desire to write songs that would reflect his own experiences.

Upon his release from prison in early 1960, Haggard was determined to turn his life around. He began working for his brother who was an electrician, while also performing at night in local bars and clubs. In 1963, he was hired by Wynn Stewart to play in his backup band; there, local promoter Fuzzy Owen heard him play and signed him to his small record label. Haggard had his first solo hit with "Sing Me a Sad Song," followed by a minor hit, a duet with Bonnie Owens called "Just Between the Two of Us." (Bonnie Owens was married to Buck Owens at the time, although she would soon leave him to marry Haggard and join his road show.) He had his first top-ten hit, "(My Friends Are Gonna Be) Strangers," in 1964; the song also gave Haggard the name for his backup band.

Following this hit, Haggard was signed to Capitol Records. His next hit, "I'm a Lonesome Fugitive," defined the classic Haggard stance: that of a man who had been in trouble with the law, but now regretted his rough-and-rowdy earlier days (although he was still subject to temptation). More prison ballads followed, including Merle's own compositions "Branded Man" and his first number-one hit, "Sing Me Back Home." His 1968 hit, "Mama Tried," told of the difficulty his mother had in raising him, expressing regret for his difficult teenage years. Haggard gained his greatest notoriety for his 1969 recording of "Okie from Muskogee," a song that cemented Haggard's position in mainstream, conservative country circles.

By the mid-'70s, Haggard's life and career were in disarray; his marriage to Bonnie Owens was on the rocks, and he broke with his long-time record label, Capitol, in 1977. He took a brief break from the music business, hinting that he would no longer perform, although he quickly reemerged as a performer and recording artist. He recorded a duet, "The Bull and the Bear," in 1978 with Leona Williams (who also cowrote the song); the two were married soon after, although the marriage lasted only until 1983. Haggard continued to tour and record over the following decades, a stubborn holdout who stayed true to his unique style and sound.

Breaking out of the Nashville mold: Willie and Waylon

While the Bakersfield singers were somewhat insulated from the grip of Nashville's record industry, singers and songwriters who went to country music's capital could not easily escape the heavy-handed approach that ruled its recording studios through

"Mama tried"

the '60s and early '70s. Breaking from Nashville's music industry, these singers forged their own style, which came to be known as "outlaw country." The outlaw movement was given a strong push by RCA when they released the compilation album *Wanted: The Outlaws* in 1976, featuring Willie Nelon, Waylon Jennings, Jessi Colter (then Jennings's wife), and Tompall Glaser. This album helped "brand" the outlaw movement and introduced a new audience—from pop and rock as well as country—to this musical style.

Texas singer Willie Nelson (who wrote the hits "Crazy" for Patsy Cline and "Hello Walls" for Faron Young, both in 1961) felt particularly constrained by the smooth production style employed on his initial recordings. Producers sought to sand away his rough edges, but Nelson instinctively knew that it was his very idiosyncratic singing and guitar playing—along with his unique approach to songwriting—that made him special.

Born in Abbot, Texas (north of Waco), Nelson was the son of a farmer and began performing while still in high school. He served in the Air Force until 1952 and then worked in Texas and briefly in Vancouver, as both a performer and country deejay. After publishing his first song, he moved to Nashville, where he joined honky-tonk singer Ray Price, as bassist in his backup band. After scoring his initial success as a songwriter, Nelson recorded in the '60s as a solo artist. However, the Nashville establishment didn't know what to make of his talents, and he sounds distinctly uncomfortable on most of these recordings.

When Nelson's house burned down in 1970, he moved to Austin, Texas, turning his back on Nashville's country music community. Influenced by younger performers who also were weary of the Nashville sound, including Kris Kristofferson and Waylon Jennings, Nelson began to experiment with writing song cycles, or groups of related songs, that would be issued on a series of seminal LPs, including 1973's *Shotgun Willie*, 1974's *Phases and*

Country Music

Stages (telling the story of the breakup of a relationship from both the man's and woman's perspectives), and 1975's landmark *Red Headed Stranger*, a romantic story set in the nineteenth-century Wild West. Nelson was given artistic control over his recordings and often pared his sound down to only his own vocals and guitar, as on his first hit, 1975's cover of Fred Rose's "Blue Eyes Crying in the Rain" from the *Stranger* concept LP. He was among the first to record with his own road band, which was particularly attuned to his unique sense of phrasing. Through the late '70s and early '80s Willie performed as a soloist and in duets with Jennings, Leon Russell, and Merle Haggard, as well as in the informal group the Highwaymen, with Johnny Cash, Kristofferson, and Jennings.

Nelson's partner in outlaw crime was singer–songwriter Waylon Jennings. Born in Littlefield, Texas, about 100 miles southwest of Amarillo, Jennings came from a musical family and was already performing on local radio when he was twelve years old. He got his first work as a deejay at the radio station in nearby Lubbock, where he met pop-rocker Buddy Holly. Holly produced his first single and invited the young singer to be his bass player on what would turn out to be his last tour. Fortunately for the future country star, Jennings gave up his seat on Holly's doomed last flight and elected to remain on the tour bus. Following Holly's death, Jennings continued to work as a deejay and recorded in a rockabilly style.

In the mid-'60s, Waylon hooked up with producer Chet Atkins at RCA Records. Although he had some minor country hits, he was unhappy with the way RCA was handling him and began introducing different material into his recordings. In 1970, he recorded a couple of songs by a then-unknown songwriter named Kris Kristofferson, including "Sunday Morning Coming Down"; a year later he released an album titled *Ladies Love Outlaws* featuring more contemporary songs. In 1972, he renegotiated with RCA, gaining artistic control over his recordings—one of the first country artists to achieve this freedom. The first album made under this new contract was 1973's *Honky Tonk Heroes*, featuring Waylon's road band, the Waylors, on a set of hard-driving songs mostly written by Billy Joe Shaver. In 1978, Jennings recorded the classic album of duets with Nelson called *Willie and Waylon*. Like that of Nelson, Jennings's later career was spent mainly on the road with his band, playing his hits for his dedicated audience.

Kris Kristofferson was always more of a songwriter than a performer, although he enjoyed some success on the country charts in the early '70s. Born in 1936 in Brownsville, Texas, Kristofferson was an Army brat who is probably the only country star to ever receive a Rhodes Scholarship to attend Oxford University. Kristofferson began performing while living in England, where he recorded as a teen pop singer under the name "Kris Carson." In 1960, he joined the Army, and on his discharge five years later he moved to Nashville. He first gained success as a songwriter, when Roger Miller recorded the original cover of "Me and Bobby McGee" and Johnny Cash covered "Sunday Morning Coming Down," both in 1969. One year later, Sammi Smith had a big hit with Kristofferson's "Help Me Make It through the Night," a particularly forthright and controversial love song for the time.

Janis Joplin's cover of "Me and Bobby McGee" just before her tragic death in 1971 helped catapult Kristofferson to pop-star status. Two years later, Gladys Knight scored a pop hit with her version of "Help Me Make It through the Night." In the same year, Kristofferson wed Rita Coolidge, also a well-known pop singer. The marriage lasted five years and produced two duo albums. A brief flirtation with Hollywood led to his appearance in several mainstream films, and in later years he joined his mentors Cash, Nelson, and Jennings in the Highwaymen.

Another figure often associated with the outlaw movement was Hank Williams Jr. (b. 1949). The son of legendary honky-tonk songwriter and performer Hank Williams, he spent much of his early career deep in his father's shadow. His manipulative mother,

Audrey, hoped to make him truly a junior version of his famous father. Hank Jr. was featured in her road shows, always performing his daddy's material. Meanwhile, his father's old record label, MGM, encouraged the younger Williams to record near letter-perfect renditions of his father's songs.

By the late '60s, Williams was bridling at the limitations of being a clone of his father. He had a number of hits in which he commented on his strange situation, including 1966's "Standing in the Shadows (of a Very Famous Man)." He also began to write songs in a plain-spoken, straightforward style and befriended the Nashville outlaws, including Nelson and Jennings, who were seeking to return country music to its purer roots. In 1974, Williams left Nashville to live in Alabama, where he recorded his breakthrough album, *Hank Williams Jr. and Friends*, featuring country rockers like Charlie Daniels. In 1977, Williams's transformation was completed when he switched from his father's label to Warner Brothers, who marketed him as a hell-raisin' country-rocker.

Williams had many hits in the late '70s and early '80s, capped by his "All My Rowdy Friends (Have Settled Down)" single and video in 1981, which featured Hank joined by country, rock, and blues musicians. Hank cultivated a born-to-boogie image, which led to albums that seemed to be recorded in hyperdrive. By the late '80s, the unstoppable party sound was beginning to wear thin, and Williams seemed to be searching for a new direction. Nonetheless, he has remained a draw for country audiences for decades.

All of these new country stars looked different than their neighbors on the charts: instead of leisure suits, they sported leather jackets; instead of crewcuts, long locks; and instead of flying the "red, white, and blue," they proudly flaunted the hippie flag of drugs, free love, and left-leaning politics. All of this helped expand country's audience beyond its traditional base and bring it into the modern era.

"I Walk the Line": The lonesome sound of Johnny Cash

Although based in Nashville from the early '60s, Johnny Cash somehow escaped being captive to the Nashville sound. Perhaps because he had first broken through as an artist on small Sun Records out of Memphis—the same label that launched the careers of Elvis Presley, Jerry Lee Lewis, and Carl Perkins—or perhaps because he next recorded for Columbia Records, which didn't have as established an approach to recording its country artists, Cash was able to forge his own unique path, combining his distinctive baritone vocals, impactful songwriting, and stripped-down sound.

Born John Ray Cash in Kingsland, Arkansas, Cash's family were poor cotton farmers who were wiped out in the Depression. Cash joined the Air Force in the early '50s and took up the guitar while stationed in Germany. On his return home, he formed a band called the Tennessee Two (Cash played rhythm guitar, while Luther Perkins played lead guitar, and bass; later, a drummer was added to make the group the Tennessee Three). The band's near-minimalist approach to accompaniment—with Cash's guitar providing a steady, repetitive rhythm that gave his music a near hypnotic energy—is immediately recognizable from Cash's very first recordings. Signed to Sun Records, Cash scored with his country classic, "I Walk the Line" (1956). Disappointed with Sun's commercial orientation, Cash signed to Columbia Records in 1959. Cash initially recorded topical songs about America's working class, American Indians, legendary figures (such as John Henry), and outlaws, with the simple backup of his own band.

Cash's big break came with his legendary live concert at California's Folsom State Prison (held in 1968), including the classic bad-man song "Folsom Prison Blues." Bob Dylan enlisted Cash's aid for his country LP, *Nashville Skyline*, in 1969, exposing him to a younger, rock and folk-pop audience. In the same year,

9. Johnny Cash and his wife June Carter perform a duet in the mid-1970s. The duo emphasized their close marriage both onstage and off.

Cash had his first solid hit with "A Boy Named Sue," a comic song written by Shel Silverstein. Through the '70s, Cash recorded more mainstream pop-country material, while also developing an acting career. He often performed with a large revue, including his wife, June Carter Cash, members of the Carter Family, and old friends like Carl Perkins.

Cash's career faded in the '80s but in the '90s he began to receive renewed attention from both the rock and country worlds for his many contributions to music. In 1992, he was inducted into the Rock and Roll Hall of Fame for his early recordings. In the mid-'90s, Cash signed with ex-rap producer Rick Rubin to Rubin's American Records label. He eventually recorded four albums under Rubin's guidance, all of which were critically and financially successful. Cash's health began to fail in the later '90s, but he continued to perform and record until nearly the end of his life. His final album release in 2002 produced a hit with its eerie cover of the Nine Inch Nails song "Hurt." Cash succumbed to complications from diabetes on September 12, 2003.

Progressive bluegrass and country rock

Younger players were drawn to play country music in the late '60s. Raised on rock, jazz, and other "modern" popular music styles, they wanted to stretch the traditional limits of older styles like bluegrass and honky-tonk to incorporate the innovations in songwriting and recording that were introduced by groups like the Beatles and singers like Bob Dylan. Thus were two new musical styles born: progressive bluegrass (or "newgrass") and country rock.

One of the first to push beyond the traditional boundaries of bluegrass was a songwriter who—like Johnny Cash—was active in Nashville in the '60s but was definitely not a typical Nashville sound performer. Banjo player and songwriter John Cowan Harford (he later added a "t" to his last name) was born in New York City, but raised in St. Louis, and was soon an active figure in the city's bluegrass scene. In 1965, he moved to Nashville in search of a country music career. Hartford signed with RCA records in the mid-'60s, recording his highly personal songs, ranging from the comic "Old Fashioned Washing Machine" (in which he imitated the sound of an ancient washer on its last legs) to the anthemic "Gentle on My Mind," which was a major hit for Glen Campbell in 1967. After a period in Southern California, Hartford returned to Nashville in 1970 and released his classic newgrass album, *Aeroplane*. Hartford's band brought together the most talented of Nashville's session musicians, including Tut Taylor (Dobro), Norman Blake (guitar), Vassar Clements (fiddle), and Randy Scruggs (bass). This band and the record influenced many other younger players to form their own bands, including Newgrass Revival.

"Mama tried"

10. John Hartford on the set of the *Smothers Brothers Comedy Hour*, where he served on the writing staff. He used this position to write himself into the introduction of the show's summer replacement, the *Glen Campbell Goodtime Hour*.

Another influential, progressive bluegrass band that came out of St. Louis centered on brothers Doug, who played banjo, and Rodney Dillard, guitarist and vocalist. The sons of an old-time fiddler who grew up surrounded by traditional dance music, they made their local debut in 1962; soon after, they relocated to California, where they were hired to portray the "Darling" family on TV's *Andy Griffith Show*. Their first two albums were a mix of traditional country and bluegrass songs along with more contemporary numbers by songwriters like Bob Dylan. In the later '60s, the band ventured more into country rock.

Finally, an influential newgrass band out of California was the Kentucky Colonels, formed around the talented brothers Clarence and Roland White. The White family hailed from rural Lewiston, Maine, but relocated to California in 1954. Clarence and Roland were performing together by the time they were both teens, appearing on local TV. By 1963, their group had evolved into the Kentucky Colonels. Clarence White became one of the most influential guitar players in bluegrass music, thanks to his mastery of flatpicking fiddle tunes. His lightning-fast picking was featured on the Colonels' third album, *Appalachian Swing*, which had a huge impact on future newgrass bands. The group folded around late 1967, when Clarence became increasingly interested in country rock. He performed on the Byrds' country rock album *Sweetheart of the Rodeo* and soon after joined the second incarnation of the group, remaining with them through 1972. When mandolinist David Grisman and fiddler Richard Greene were asked to form a bluegrass band to perform on a local TV show, they enlisted White and singer/guitarist Peter Rowan to form Muleskinner. This band recorded one album that was highly influential on the development of newgrass later in the decade.

While bluegrass had an impact on some country musicians, perhaps more influential in the long term was a new style that came to be known as country rock. Several performers have claimed the mantle of being the first to meld country and rock music into this new style. Rick Nelson, the former '50s teen idol, was among the first to cut all-country albums and formed his

Stone Canyon Band to further his country rock sound in 1969. The Everly Brothers—who had true country roots—also dabbled in country rock on two '60s albums. However, probably the first and most important country rock LP was the Byrds' 1968 release, *Sweetheart of the Rodeo*. The album featured country standards, along with compositions by Bob Dylan and new band member Gram Parsons in a country style, performed by the band along with some of the better, younger Nashville session men. While this version of the Byrds was short-lived, the album they recorded became a model for later country rock ensembles.

A year later, Bob Dylan gave the movement added legitimacy by releasing his *Nashville Skyline* LP, in which he took on the voice of a mellow-sounding country crooner and performed a duet with Johnny Cash. Young Nashville residents like multi-instrumentalist Norman Blake and steel guitarist Pete Drake were used for these sessions; these musicians knew country roots, but were influenced by more progressive sounds. Another influential LP was Ringo Starr's *Beaucoups of Blues* recorded in Nashville in 1971; Ringo had sung Buck Owens's "Act Naturally" in the Beatles, and somehow his sad-sack vocals perfectly fit mainstream country songs. Steel guitarist Pete Drake approached Starr with the project and produced all of the tracks using Nashville's young talent.

After *Sweetheart of the Rodeo* was completed, Gram Parsons and Chris Hillman wanted to take the country rock experiment further, so they formed the Flying Burrito Brothers. Their first two LPs, made while Parsons was still with the group, are considered classics today, combining traditional country subject matter and style with a decidedly new sound. When Parsons left the band, he had a short solo career before his untimely death; he helped launch the career of country rock vocalist Emmylou Harris.

Born in Birmingham, Harris attended the University of North Carolina and formed a folk duo there. In 1969, Harris traveled to

New York's Greenwich Village and recorded her first solo album. In the early '70s, she moved to California, where she met Gram Parsons. The two became romantically and musically involved, and Harris added harmony vocals to Parsons's solo LPs and performances. After Parsons's death, Harris became a champion of country rock. Through the '70s, Harris employed many musicians who would later become well known on their own, including Rodney Crowell, Ricky Skaggs, and Vince Gill. Beginning in the '80s, Harris focused on the country audience almost exclusively. In 1987, she released *Trio* in collaboration with Linda Ronstadt and Dolly Parton, a country-flavored album that yielded her biggest commercial hits. Despite some occasional returns to a more rock-oriented style, Harris has continued to be an icon in country circles, inspiring countless other female performers.

Country rock not only opened country music to a new audience—namely, the young, highly literate audience for contemporary rock—but it also helped remind country of its roots in Western swing, honky-tonk, and bluegrass, while pointing the way to a new music that could be based on these roots. The country rock revival led, in turn, to interest in other types of country music, such as the early '80s revival of rockabilly. And all of this fed into what would become the roots country movement of the '80s and the rise of new stars like Randy Travis, Patty Loveless, and George Strait.

7

"Friends in low places": Retro-country and country-pop since 1980

The return to country roots that began in the 1980s continues in the early twenty-first century, in reaction both to the demise of countrypolitan and the influence of the country outlaws. Honky-tonk revivalists like George Strait, Randy Travis, and Alan Jackson helped return traditional country themes of lovin', cheatin', drinkin', and hell-raisin' to the top of the country charts. Perhaps most revolutionary of these new stars was Garth Brooks, who modernized the subjects addressed in country music as well as the music's presentation onstage, borrowing from rock and mainstream performers.

Women also came to the fore in the new country world, ranging from traditionalists like Patty Loveless to hell-raisers like Gretchen Wilson to singer–songwriters like Mary Chapin Carpenter, Lucinda Williams, and Gillian Welch, stars of the new "Americana" movement. Female groups like the Dixie Chicks helped push an empowered, liberated message both through the fact that they played their own instruments (traditionally the domain of male backup performers) and through the content of their songs, which went well beyond the traditional kitchen-and-bedroom topics. Still others, like Shania Twain and Taylor Swift, flirted closely with pop-rock sounds, to the point where they appeared to be "country" performers only in name.

Back to the honky-tonk

Just as Texas was the home of the outlaw movement in the 1970s and '80s, it remained a hotbed for traditional country styles over the decades—particularly at the many dance halls and small bars that dotted the rural areas of the state. One star who worked his way up through the dance hall and bar circuit was George Strait, who has enjoyed a remarkable career over more than thirty years in country music.

Strait was born in rural Poteet, Texas, a tiny town located about thirty miles southwest of San Antonio, the son of a junior-high-school teacher who also raised cattle on the side. Like others of his generation, he began his career playing rock and pop music. After serving in the Army, he began performing locally with the group Ace in the Hole and recorded for the tiny D label out of Houston. He hit Nashville in the late '70s, but failed to find a recording contract until 1981. His first album, *Strait Country*, established his signature southwestern sound, which recalled the best of the early '50s honky-tonkers, including Hank Thompson, Ray Price, and Faron Young. Strait also scored a top-ten hit with his first single, "Unwound." He continued to hit it big through the '80s, covering Bob Wills's classic "Right or Wrong" and Whitey Shafer's "Does Fort Worth Ever Cross Your Mind?" His novelty hit, "All My Ex's Live in Texas," even got some pop radio play. Despite a brief foray into more "urban" country sounds in the early '90s, Strait's hits over the ensuing decades find him stylistically almost frozen in time. He continued to be a major concert draw up through his two-year-long "Cowboy Rides Again Tour" from 2012 to 2014, which he said would mark the end of his live performances.

Another major country star of the 1980s was Randy Travis (b. Randy Bruce Traywick). Born in Marshville, North Carolina, located about forty miles southeast of Charlotte, Travis began playing guitar at age eight, and by the time he was a teenager, he was performing as a duo with his brother in local clubs. When he was sixteen, he ran away from home and won a talent contest in Charlotte, which led to his discovery by local bar owner Lib Hatcher, the manager who would support his career for seven years before he hit it big (later, the duo married).

Performing under the name Randy Ray, he went to Nashville with Hatcher at the age of twenty-three. He soon took the stage name of "Travis," in honor of legendary country singer and guitarist Merle Travis. He signed with Warner Brothers records, releasing his most memorable album, *Storms of Life*, in 1986. Randy's hits off this first LP have the sly edge of the best country music; songs like "On the Other Hand" and "Digging Up Bones" play on classic country themes of lovin', losin', and cheatin', but with humorous undertones that are perfectly paired with Randy's deadpan delivery. Randy scored numerous hits through the mid-'90s, but none had the adventuresome quality of his first recordings. However, Travis's career cooled as newer stars dominated the charts, and he later turned to performing gospel music.

The retro-country revival of the '80s that was heralded by artists like Strait and Travis took its visual cues from an earlier generation of cowboy-hat-wearing country stars. Unlike the spray tans and leisure suits that were popularized by countrypolitan stars like Kenny Rogers, stars of the 1980s dressed like "real cowboys," projecting the image of farm-raised country boys. A slew of younger male imitators would follow who came to be nicknamed the "hunks in hats" for both their beefy masculine visual appeal and their adherence to country's beloved imagery and musical styles.

Among the first new country stars in this mold was Alan Jackson. Born in Newnan, Georgia (just outside of Atlanta), Jackson's story is the kind of rags-to-riches odyssey that Nashville loves. Having married young, he worked as a forklift driver while writing songs in his spare time. His wife was his biggest supporter and urged him to relocate to Nashville. A chance meeting with Glen Campbell at the Nashville airport led to a job as a songwriter with Campbell's publisher. In 1989, Jackson released his first album, featuring nine of his original songs. Jackson's vocal style owes much to his mentor, George Jones, and the other great '50s honky-tonk singers. His recordings are tastefully produced in a new country style and range from old-fashioned weepers to modern dance numbers. His spunky "Don't Rock the Jukebox," a 1991 rockabilly-flavored number, declared Jackson's allegiance to traditional country sounds. His 1993 summer hit, "Chatahoochee," offers a nostalgic reminiscence of a country youth.

Unlike other early '90s stars who have faded from the scene, Jackson managed to continue to produce hits, without changing his style much. His 2001 hit, "It's Alright to Be a Redneck," could have been featured on his first album. In late 2001, Jackson released the somewhat maudlin pop ballad, "Where Were You (When the World Stopped Turning)," recorded following the attacks on the World Trade Center and Pentagon. Since then, Jackson has proven that—like many earlier country musicians— the country audience will support a performer long after his chart-topping days are over.

Other hit-making male performers were drawn from the world of newgrass and country rock. Included among those players were master guitarist and singer Vince Gill, who cut his teeth playing in bluegrass bands and then worked with the country rock outfit Pure Prairie League; and mandolin master Ricky Skaggs, who enjoyed a brief burst of popularity on the country charts before returning to his lifelong love, bluegrass music. Countless other hunky hat-wearers continued to dominate the charts through the early twenty-first century, including twangy guitar masters Brad Paisley and Keith Urban, who blended retro-rock guitar lines with classic country themes.

Country megastars: Garth Brooks, Tim McGraw, and Faith Hill

The most successful of this new generation of neo-honky-tonk heroes was Garth Brooks, who supersized country music to fill major stadiums. Like the favorite 7-11 drink the Big Gulp, Brooks specialized in oversized emotions, whether swinging from the rafters on stage or singing an emotionally drenched ballad that never failed to bring tears to his eyes. His audience was happy to go along for the ride.

Brooks was born in Tulsa, Oklahoma; his father worked in the oil industry and his mother Colleen had a minor career as a country singer, appearing on the local *Ozark Mountain Jamboree* broadcast. Brooks's guitar-playing career began in high school and continued in college. On a trip to Nashville in 1987, he attracted the attention of producer Allen Reynolds. Brooks's first album was successful, producing the number-one country hit "If Tomorrow Never Comes." However, his 1990 followup, *No Fences*, was a phenomenon: it sold 700,000 copies in its first ten days of release and stayed on the pop charts for over a year. It contained huge hits including the pop ballad "The Dance" and the joyous honky-tonk number "Friends in Low Places." Brooks even tackled themes not normally addressed in country music, such as spousal abuse in the song "The Thunder Rolls." Follow-up singles showed Brooks veering between rock-like performances and more "sensitive" ballads. Throughout the 1990s, he was nearly bulletproof, riding both the country and pop charts as easily as a buckaroo on the range.

Brooks's life and music took a tabloid turn in the late '90s when he remade himself as the fictional pop singer "Chris Gaines," both on record and in a proposed film; the album was released first and was so poorly received that the film was never shown. Brooks withdrew from the public eye in 2000, amid announcements that

"Friends in low places"

his long-time marriage to his first wife was coming to an end. But never one to give up easily, Brooks came roaring back with his album *Scarecrow* in the autumn of 2001. Announced as his "last" album, it returned him to the sound and style of his earlier country outings, and the fans responded by making it a major hit. Since then, Brooks has occasionally returned to performing and recording, continuing to draw on his early career hits.

Brooks's success in the '90s was equaled by the country power couple of Tim McGraw and Faith Hill. McGraw was born in Delhi, Louisiana (near the Mississippi border). He descends from baseball royalty: his father, Tug McGraw, had an affair with his mother, a fact that was not revealed to McGraw until he was a teen. To that point, he was raised as "Tim Smith," the unassuming son of a trucker. Arriving in Nashville in 1989, Tim scuffled along until Tug arranged for a friend at Curb Records to listen to his son's audition tape, and McGraw was signed to the label in 1991.

After releasing a debut album in 1992 that saw little action, McGraw leapt to prominence with the release of 1994's aptly titled *Not a Moment Too Soon*. The bestselling country album of the year, it yielded two gold singles ("Indian Outlaw" and "Don't Take the Girl") in less than three months. The hits kept coming with the release of his third album, *All I Want*, in 1995, with Tim balancing romantic ballads (including the title track) with more uptempo rockers ("I Like It, I Love It"). Following its release, McGraw set out on a summer tour, selecting up-and-coming country singer Faith Hill as his opening act. A romance blossomed, and the two were wed in 1996.

Cashing in on their romantic attachment, McGraw and Hill released their first vocal duet, "It's Your Love," which was the lead release from McGraw's fourth album, 1997's *Everywhere*. The song spent six weeks in the number-one spot, a record for *Billboard*'s country charts, and launched further McGraw-mania. In 1999, McGraw released *A Place in the Sun*, which continued the formula of bad-boy uptempo numbers and tearful ballads, producing five hit singles, including two number-one hits ("Please Remember Me" and "Something Like That"). The album debuted at number one on both the pop and country charts—no small achievement. Another duet with Hill—"Let's Make Love"—brought McGraw his first Grammy. By the turn of the twenty-first century, McGraw had sold over 19 million albums and nearly 5 million singles, eclipsing Garth Brooks as the biggest male name in country music. His hits continued into the 2000s, with power ballads like "Live Like You Were Dying" in 2004.

McGraw's wife, Audrey Faith Perry, was born in Jackson, Mississippi, but raised outside of the city. She began singing at church and local functions. Determined to make it as a singer–songwriter, she moved to Nashville in her late teens, where she was hired for a desk job at a music-publishing company; this led to work singing on demo recordings, which in turn led to a job as a backup singer for Gary Burr, who subsequently produced Hill's first album.

Hill's first single, "Wild One," promoted by a sexy video, shot to number one; Hill's debut album, *Take Me as I Am*, went gold in 1994 and subsequently double platinum. Her big breakthrough came in 1998 with the hit song "This Kiss," a sugary pop confection, and the album from which the single was drawn, *Faith*, went platinum in little over a month after its release. Hill crossed over from country superstardom to pop diva status in 1999 with the release of her album *Breathe*. The title track became Hill's first platinum seller, topping country, pop, and adult contemporary charts. The album produced four major hits, including the title track, "The Way You Love Me" and "If My Heart Had Wings."

Both McGraw and Hill have had continued success in the twenty-first century, although mostly as touring acts, whether alone or as a duo. This fits the typical Nashville pattern for country performers, who can have long careers on the road long after their chart-topping days are over.

The return of country women

The country hunks were successful in part because the country audience was primarily made up of women. Although they flocked to hear male singers, they also wanted to hear songs performed by members of their own sex that addressed issues unique to their side of the classic country equation of love gone wrong. This opened the door for a wide variety of bestselling female performers during this period.

Singer Patty Loveless was one of the first female stars to break out in a big way in the new country style. Born Patty Ramey in Pikeville, Kentucky, to a coal miner, Loveless was first introduced to country music through her older brother, Roger, who later managed her career. She began performing as a duo with him at age twelve. Roger took her to Nashville two years later, where she was hired to replace her cousin, Loretta Lynn, in the Wilburn Brothers summer touring show. She toured for several summers with them, eventually marrying their drummer, Terry Lovelace. After her wedding, she went into semiretirement in North Carolina.

Patty returned to Nashville in the mid-'80s after her marriage failed and changed her stage name to "Loveless" (to avoid confusion with the porn actress Linda Lovelace). For her debut LP, she recorded a mix of new country styles by leading singer–songwriters of the Nashville scene. Some of her early hits included the ballad "I Did," from her first album, and uptempo numbers like "Timber I'm Falling in Love" and "I'm That Kind of Girl" (both with a rocking edge). Loveless had a hard time producing hits through the later '90s, as younger (and more video-friendly) female singers came to the fore. She scored her last major country hits in 1995 with "Lonely Too Long" and "You Can Feel Bad." Like many in her generation, she remade herself as a bluegrass singer later in the decade. She has more or less retired from the music scene in the twenty-first century, although she continues to sing occasionally on the *Grand Ole Opry*.

Reba McEntire began her career as a new-country star before transitioning to a country diva with one foot in the pop-music world. Born in Chockie, Oklahoma, McEntire comes from an authentic rodeo family; her grandfather was a celebrity on the national rodeo circuit and her father a talented roper. Her brother, Pake, and two sisters, Alice and Susie, all performed in rodeos, as did young Reba, and the four formed a family singing group, scoring a local hit in 1971 with a ballad memorializing their grandfather, "The Ballad of John McEntire." Country star Red Steagall heard Reba sing the national anthem at the National Rodeo Finals in Oklahoma City in 1974 and invited her to come to Nashville to make a demo. Reba, her mother, and her brother Pake all ended up in Music City, and both brother and sister made their first albums in late 1975.

Reba's first recordings were in a traditional style, and although they forecast the new country trends of the next decade, they failed to find much chart action. In the late '70s and early '80s, she finally began to see some success, covering Patsy Cline's "Sweet Dreams" and "A Poor Man's Roses"; her first number-one record came in 1983 with "Can't Even Get the Blues." This launched a series of hits throughout the decade.

In 1987, McEntire divorced her first husband; two years later she married her steel guitarist and road manager, Narvel Blackstock. The newly married duo began building McEntire's empire, managing and booking her act, and working with the record company and producers to shape her image. She also began to pursue an acting career, landing some minor TV roles in miniseries and movies, but her best acting remained in her videos, in which she continued to project a feisty, yet down-home and lovable, personality.

The '90s saw McEntire continue to be a strong concert draw, while her recordings consistently sold well. In 1999, celebrating her 40-millionth record sold, the Recording Industry of America named her "Female Country Artist of the Century." She has become popular as a TV sitcom star and also as a host of various country music award shows.

As younger singers and performers arrived in Nashville, new showcases arose, such as the Bluebird Café, to support their more progressive approach to singing and songwriting. Support organizations by and for these musicians arose as a means of both honoring country roots and acknowledging the need to address new topics and incorporate new instruments and sounds. One of the most prominent (although short-lived) of these groups was the so-called Muzik Mafia, which centered on the singers, performers, and producers Big and Rich. The duo enjoyed some success in the early 2000s and helped launch the career of the "hell-raisin'," take-no-prisoners singer Gretchen Wilson. Wilson was one of many singer–songwriters who were drawn to Nashville to try to establish themselves as performers, but could not crack through the hidebound, traditional gatekeepers in the recording and publishing industries. She showed up at a "meeting" (more like an informal gathering and song-swap) of the Mafia and was instantly recognized by Big and Rich as a woman who could bring a rock sensibility to country music and thus appeal to a younger generation of listeners. Wilson had her biggest hits straight out of the box with 2004's hyperpumped anthems "Redneck Woman" and "Here for the Party." While her tough-as-nails image helped quickly make her a star, Wilson had trouble escaping its limitations. Nonetheless, her accomplishments would lead to the success of future stars like Miranda Lambert.

Lambert hails from Longview, Texas, where her parents initially worked as private detectives until they became faith ministers. During her high school years, Lambert played and sang locally, where she was "discovered" by a local promoter. She came to

Nashville at age eighteen, but was discouraged by the material given to her by producers to record. She insisted on cutting her own material, scoring big in 2003 with the album and single *Kerosene*, which solidified her tough-girl image. This was continued through her follow-up hits, including "Gunpowder 'n' Lead" and others through the early 2000s. She also formed a group with fellow singer–songwriters Ashley Monroe and Angaleena Presley, the Pistol Annies, which recorded the tongue-in-cheek anthem "Hell on Heels" in 2011. Lambert's success continued into the new millennium, with the archly named album *Platinum* in 2014 (a play on both her blond hair and the industry's term for a million-selling album) and *The Weight of These Wings* (2016). Lambert continued to cultivate the "tough-gal-with-a-heart-of-gold" image in her touring shows and songs that featured favorite country themes, including "Smokin' and Drinkin'" and "Vice."

While men could easily slip between macho honky-tonk music and teary ballads, women had a harder time bridging this gap. Wilson stuck to the hard-edged sound, while others like Lee Ann Womack revived a countrypolitan-influenced style with ballads with greeting-card sentiments such as "I Hope You Dance." For a while, the Dixie Chicks—a group formed around sisters Martie Erwin Maguire on fiddle and Emily Erwin Robison on banjo, along with vocalist Natalie Maines—managed to successfully bridge this gap, with hit power ballads like "Wide Open Spaces" and "Cowboy Take Me Away" and harder-edged material like the tongue-in-cheek "Goodbye Earl," a song about an abusive husband who is killed by his long-suffering wife. The Chicks eventually were embroiled with fights with their record label and political controversies—notably, they denounced president George W. Bush for his decision to go to war in Iraq in 2003—that derailed their commercial career.

Almost like family: Country harmony groups

Since the brother acts of the 1930s, harmony singing has been a key element of commercial country music. The first duo to revive the older harmony tradition was the mother–daughter act, the Judds. Naomi Judd (b. Diana Ellen Judd) gave birth to her daughter, Christina Ciminella (later Wynonna Judd), in Ashland, Kentucky. Wynonna's father soon disappeared, and Naomi took her family to California, where she tried, unsuccessfully, to become a model. In the mid-'70s, the family returned to Kentucky, where Wynonna began to show her budding talent on the guitar, and mother and daughter began singing together. In 1979, they moved to Nashville, where Naomi pursued a nursing degree while the duo recorded demo tapes on a thirty-dollar recorder purchased at Kmart. In 1983, they successfully auditioned for RCA records, leading to a recording contract.

The first Judds recordings were very much in the mold of traditional country harmony singing, and the arrangements

11. In this early publicity photo, the Judds, Wynonna (left) and her mother Naomi (right), sport nearly identical clothing, makeup, and hairdos, resembling twins rather than a mother–daughter act.

emphasized acoustic instruments without too much clutter. Their first number-one hit played off their mother–daughter relationship, in "Mama He's Crazy" (1984). A string of hits came through the '80s, including the sentimental "Grandpa (Tell Me 'Bout the Good Old Days)," the uptempo "Rockin' with the Rhythm of the Rain," and the anthemic "Love Can Build a Bridge." These songs showed the talents of Wynonna as a gutsy lead singer, tempered by her mother's sweet harmonies. As their career grew, their recordings became more heavily produced and their act more elaborate. However, the Nashville music world was stunned by the announcement of Naomi's retirement from active performing, due to chronic hepatitis, in 1990; the duo undertook a yearlong "farewell tour," culminating in a pay-per-view concert at the end of 1991. Wynonna came out from under her mother's shadow with her first solo LP, showing the influence of pop-rock singers, particularly Bonnie Raitt, on her style, but her career pretty much ended in the later '90s.

Vocal harmony groups that drew their style from country rock came to prominence in the '80s through the '90s, including such hitmakers as Diamond Rio and the Sawyer Brown Band. Other harmony groups have taken a softer approach. Since the turn of the twenty-first century, bands like Lady Antebellum, Little Big Town, and Rascal Flatts have had major hits performing in a style reminiscent of California country rock outfits such as the Eagles. Rascal Flatts come closest to being a pure pop band, sounding much like the popular "boy bands" that dominated the charts in the '90s. More recently, country rocker Zac Brown (who broke country rules by sporting a dockworker's wooly pull-down cap rather than the traditional cowboy headwear) and new groups like Midland and Levon (named in honor of Levon Helm of the Band) have combined smooth harmonies with a rock-and-roll sound and instrumentation.

One of the most successful of these bands was Lady Antebellum, who won the non-genre-specific Grammy awards in 2010 for Song of the Year and Record of the Year for their crossover success "'Need You Now." Although band member Charles Kelley claimed that in writing and recording the song the group "had no intentions of this ever crossing over," it is clearly a power-pop ballad that could have been comfortably recorded years earlier by singers like Celine Dion. Country artists have to claim allegiance to the genre while simultaneously seeking mainstream success, so it may be that Kelley protested a bit too much.

Country singer–songwriters

Country music has always shadowed trends in popular music at large, often adopting popular styles about a decade after their initial success. This is particularly apparent in the number of female singer–songwriters who came to the fore in the '80s and '90s. Some were strongly influenced by songwriters like Joni Mitchell and Carole King, who greatly expanded the topics that could be addressed in popular song to include thorny issues raised through the women's liberation movement. Of these performers, Mary Chapin Carpenter was the most successful, although her period topping the country charts was brief.

The daughter of a *Life* magazine executive, Carpenter was born and raised in suburban Princeton, New Jersey. Her mother had played the guitar during the early '60s and gave her instrument to Carpenter when she expressed interest in learning it. Her family moved to Washington, DC, in 1974, and after college, Carpenter began performing in the Washington area. She hooked up with guitarist John Jennings, and the duo produced a demo tape that led to an audition for Columbia, which signed Carpenter and released her first LP in 1987.

From 1987 to 1992, Carpenter developed a cult following. She scored a minor hit with 1989's "How Do," a flirtation song told from a woman's point of view. But her breakthrough came with the Cajun-flavored hit 1992 single, "Down at the Twist and Shout." She quickly followed up with her 1993 releases, "I Feel Lucky," another uptempo number, and her cover of Lucinda Williams's "Passionate Kisses." Her "He Thinks He'll Keep Her" was a tongue-in-cheek song that told of a woman finally getting the courage to leave her long-time husband, who had been oblivious to her dreams of having a life beyond housework. Carpenter's Ivy League heritage and sophisticated humor were clearly not in line with the more hard-core elements of the country audience, and her later work was dropped by country radio.

Several other women have walked the line between country stardom and what is often called "Americana" or alt-country music. Lucinda Williams—the author of Chapin Carpenter's hit "Passionate Kisses"—has never really been a country star, despite incorporating strong doses of honky-tonk into her music. Gillian Welch has taken a different approach, going so retro that she sounds like an escapee from the Dust Bowl, performing her stark songs with simple acoustic guitar accompaniments—despite being raised in Los Angeles, California. The return to roots country was given a major boost by the success of the 2000 film *O Brother, Where Art Thou?*, which featured performances by Welch, bluegrass singer Alison Krauss, and Emmylou Harris, among others.

Country? Pop? Something else?

While the revival of country traditions in the '80s seemed to be pointing to a new golden era for fans of country's heyday, in fact many artists who began in the "country" camp began to feel the irresistible pull of mass success and popularity. "Modernizing" the country sound came to mean inviting in producers more associated with rock, pop, and even R&B and rap. While one can debate whether the outcome represented a positive or negative move for country as a whole, by the dawn of the twenty-first century it was clear that country and popular music were in many ways one and the same thing.

Two changes in the way the music industry measured popularity helped upend some common assumptions that had determined the direction of commercial music for decades. Traditional methods of accounting for record sales were notoriously inaccurate, and numbers were often inflated by the labels themselves to hype their releases. Less attention was paid to country releases than to so-called top-ten or pop records, which were long assumed to be bigger moneymakers. When electronic point-of-sale scanning was introduced in the '80s, much of the industry was surprised to see that the actual sales of country records were much larger than previously assumed. In fact, some country records were more "popular" than those that were marketed as "pop" recordings. The growth of digital downloads in the '90s, and then streaming, provided further evidence of country's popularity. With no need to visit a physical record store (and perhaps suffer the embarrassment of buying a country release in public), consumers voted with their iPods and cell phones and flocked to country releases.

Country had always been popular as a radio format, and the success of the new country stars of the 1980s and '90s led many stations that previously focused on adult contemporary or top-ten music to convert to country. In the latest industry tallies, country stations far outstrip any other musical style, with over 1,800 stations nationwide, making it number one for all radio formats (news radio is number two at about 1,300 stations). Seeing these numbers, the music industry as a whole upped its investment in country acts.

It wasn't long before a number of would-be pop stars realized that switching to performing country music might give them a leg up in breaking into mainstream success. The first singer to really exploit this new world was Canadian-born Shania Twain. She was born Eileen Edwards in 1965, in the small, backwoods town of Timmins, Ontario, Canada. She began singing at the age of three, winning talent shows from the age of eight, and performing locally

and on national television from her early teen years. She trained
as a Broadway-style singer, dancer, and performer and found
professional work at a Canadian resort performing in a Vegas-
style revue. However, after her mother and stepfather were
tragically killed in an automobile accident, she decided to jump on
the country bandwagon, moving to Nashville in 1991.

Twain was quickly signed to Mercury Records, hitting it big with
her sexy video presence on her first single, "Whose Bed Have Your
Boots Been Under." The album produced more hits, including
"Any Man of Mine" and "(If You're Not in It for Love) I'm Out of
Here." All of the songs were marked by a spunky forthrightness in
their lyrics that appealed strongly to women, while their sexy
underpinnings—and basically romantic and nonthreatening
messages—made the songs attractive to men. The album teamed
her with pop-rock producer Robert "Mutt" Lange, who had been
previously the mastermind behind hard rockers AC/DC. Lange
coauthored many of her hits and was soon her husband. The duo
returned big time with Twain's 1997 album, *Come on Over*.
Although a "country" album in name, it was really mainstream
pop in the style of singers like Gloria Estefan or Celine Dion. The
album was a massive seller, producing many top hits, including
the big ballads "You're Still the One" and "From This Moment"
and the spunky "That Don't Impress Me Much," "Don't Be Stupid,"
and "Man! I Feel Like a Woman," which subsequently was used in
an advertising campaign by Revlon featuring Twain. The album
has broken all records, selling over 18 million copies,
spawning eight hit singles, and becoming, by *Billboard*'s
estimation, the bestselling recording by a female artist of all
time, in any genre.

Perhaps realizing that Twain's music was straddling two different
audiences, her next album, 2002's *Up*, was released in three
versions: American buyers received two CDs, one mixed for the
country market, the other for pop; and Europeans received a
unique mix of their own, plus the pop mix. The album's first

single, "I'm Gonna Getcha," was an immediate number-one hit on country and pop charts. It was followed by more top hits, including "Forever and For Always" and "She's Not Just a Pretty Face." However, both her professional partnership and marriage with Lange ended soon thereafter, and Twain's career ground to a halt. Nonetheless, she had created a roadmap for other singers to follow.

Country has always been receptive to teen (and even preteen) women who straddle the line between innocence and maturity. Tanya Tucker—who scored big with the suggestive hits "Delta Dawn" and "Would You Lay with Me (in a Field of Stone)" when she was twelve years old—was among the first to play on this "sexy-but-sweet" image. Tucker was a role model for future country stars, including thirteen-year-old LeAnn Rimes, whose big-lunged rendition of "Blue" and other songs reminiscent of Patsy Cline's later style launched her career. So it's not surprising that one of the biggest country stars of the turn of the twenty-first century also began her career as a teenager. But, unlike Tucker and Rimes, who only flirted with the pop charts, this newcomer would use country music as a stepping-stone to a career in mainstream pop.

Taylor Swift grew up in suburban Pennsylvania, the daughter of middle-class parents. At age nine, she began to take singing lessons, aspiring for a career in musical theater. However, inspired by Shania Twain's mid-'90s hits, she set her eye on country music, talking her mother into taking her to Nashville as an early teen to audition for the major labels. Although she was not initially successful, Swift soon learned to play the guitar and began writing her own material, and by the time she was ready to attend high school, she had convinced her father to relocate the family to the Nashville suburbs. There she began working with professional songwriters to hone her craft and appeared at artist showcases. At age fourteen, she was signed to a record deal, and her debut album followed two years later. Cannily, the first single she released was titled "Tim McGraw," relating her supposed infatuation with the major country star, which established her bona fide with the country audience.

Swift's two follow-up albums, *Fearless* and *Speak Now*, were marketed as country releases, but each sold widely to a pop audience. Swift's songs addressed typical pop music themes of love, betrayal, and female empowerment, and the arrangements increasingly sounded more like mainstream pop. But it was the release of *1989* in 2014 that most strongly indicated her aim to be a pop star. Symbolically, she moved that same year from Nashville to New York City. Swift became one of the few—and most successful—female performers to effectively move beyond the confines of the country format. Today, few even recall her years as a country performer.

While some country performers and critics saw Swift's *1989* album as a betrayal of the music, others saw her opening doors to new listeners. Miranda Lambert—another figure who straddles country and pop—noted that "[Swift] really helped country music....Some people still think that country music is twangy and cheesy, and they pigeonhole us....But I thought, If they're looking for Taylor's videos or songs...they might like me too." The tension between the purists and those who seek to expand country's reach has always been a part of country's story, and not surprisingly, that continues today.

Perhaps a more typical example of a country star going pop is Blake Shelton. Born in Ada, Oklahoma, like many other future country stars, Shelton began writing songs and performing as a teenager, leaving his hometown at age eighteen in the hopes of finding success in Nashville. Befriended by older country star Bobby Braddock, who also produced Shelton's first album, the singer had his first hit with "Austin" in 2001, which topped the country charts for five weeks—a record for a debut single shared by only one other artist, Billy Ray Cyrus with his 1992 "Achy

Breaky Heart." Shelton's style is fairly generic, twenty-first century country, lyrically conservative with mainstream pop-rock flavored accompaniments. After scoring additional hits through the mid-2000s, Shelton was hired to be a judge on the reality show *Nashville Star* (a copycat show based on the success of *American Idol*), increasing his fame. In 2010 he was made a member of the *Grand Ole Opry* and a year later became a "vocal consultant" for *The Voice*, a hit, pop-oriented vocal competition show that he would later join as a full judge. Shelton has managed to be both a country star and a pop star, showing again the rather porous relationship between these musical styles in the new century.

While other country acts have not been quite as determined to leave the countrified hills of Nashville for the big-city glamor of New York, it is clear that today's country music bears much in common with what a few decades ago would have been considered mainstream pop. Does the label "country music" mean anything anymore? It's hard to say.

Coda: Country music in a new millennium

Throughout its history, country performers have always balanced two contradictory impulses: on the one hand, they value their musical influences and the many earlier styles that have made the music what it is today; on the other, they are interested in adding to the tradition by incorporating the latest technical and musical innovations. The same tension has occurred in jazz, rock, and other popular styles; there are those who wish to preserve the music against any changes, while there are others who welcome outside influences.

In the twenty-first century, we see the same scenario playing out among the latest country stars. Neotraditionalists like Jon Pardi—with his 2016 number-one hit "Dirt on My Boots"—and Chris Stapleton—who once led a progressive bluegrass band and now plays a mix of hard country, rock, blues, and a smattering of bluegrass—have shown how traditional styles can remain dynamic in a new age. Sturgill Simpson is perhaps the most innovative of the traditionalists, beginning his career very much in the outlaw mold, but since incorporating everything from psychedelic rock to heavy metal in his performances and recordings. At the same time, he ruffled Nashville feathers in 2016 by publishing a rambling essay on his Facebook page criticizing the country music industry for failing to honor its elders.

On the other end of the spectrum are groups like Florida Georgia Line (the duo of Tyler Hubbard and Brian Kelley), whose 2016 album *Dig Your Roots* focuses not on country's roots per se, but rather on the duo's own interests in everything from country to reggae and boy bands. Their music is said to have launched the "bro country" movement, featuring songs with hypermacho lyrics and themes accompanied by heavy rocking accompaniments. Singers like Maren Morris (whose initial single, 2015's "My Church," was a major country and pop hit) show the influence of pop performers like Mariah Carey and many other R&B divas. Perhaps the biggest indication that pop and country are becoming increasingly one and the same was the appearance of Beyoncé at the Country Music Awards in 2016, where she performed her song "Daddy Lessons," accompanied by the Dixie Chicks. Country diehards were scandalized, but the mainstream country audience accepted this performance as just one more expression on the spectrum of what can be called "country music."

Of course, the country charts represent only one element of the richness of the music. Many country stars who were at one time the latest "hot" hitmakers continue to tour for decades, drawing respectable audiences for their live shows. While some adjust their music to fit the times, others continue to perform pretty much in the same style year after year—and yet the size of their audience doesn't seem to diminish. You need only visit Nashville's annual Fan Fair to see how certain acts continue to have devoted followers long after their chart-busting days are over. And then there are artists like Willie Nelson or Dolly Parton whose music transcends changes in styles; these artists "sound" unique no matter how their music is packaged.

We return to our opening image of the pickup truck as being central to country identity. Just as twenty-first century pickup trucks have been redesigned to be more aerodynamic and efficient, so country music has been reimagined by a new

Country Music

generation of performers. The truck still hauls the goods, even as it may appear to be totally different than earlier styles. And so country music keeps trucking along, putting more mileage under its belt, despite many transformations and changes over the years.

Further reading

Bufwack, Mary A., and Robert K. Oermann. *Finding Her Voice: Women in Country Music*. New York: Crown, 1993.

Cantwell, Robert. *Bluegrass Breakdown: The Making of the Old Southern Sound*. Urbana: University of Illinois Press, 1984.

Carlin, Bob. *Banjo: An Illustrated History*. Montclair, NJ: Backbeat Books, 2016.

Carlin, Bob. *The Birth of the Banjo: Joel Walker Sweeney and Early Minstrelsy*. Jefferson, NC: McFarland, 2007.

Carlin, Richard. *Country Music*. New York: Blackdog and Leventhal, 2005.

Carlin, Richard. *Country Music: A Biographical Dictionary*. New York: Routledge, 2002.

Carlin, Richard, and Bob Carlin. *Southern Exposure: The Story of Southern Music in Pictures and Words*. New York: Billboard, 2000.

Cash, Johnny, with Patrick Carr. *Cash: The Autobiography*. New York: Harper, 1998.

Ching, Barbara. *Wrong's What I Do Best: Hard Country Music and Contemporary Culture*. New York: Oxford University Press, 2001.

Country Music Foundation Staff. *Country Music Hall of Fame and Museum Book*. Rev. ed. Nashville: Country Music Foundation, 1987.

Country Music Foundation Staff. *Country: The Music and the Musicians*. New York: Abbeville Press, 1988.

Daniel, Wayne. *Pickin' on Peachtree: A History of Country Music in Atlanta, Georgia*. Urbana: University of Illinois Press, 2000.

Dawidoff, Nicholas. *In the Country of Country: A Journey to the Roots of American Music*. New York: Vintage, 2011.

Ellison, Curtis. *Country Music Culture: From Hard Times to Heaven*.
New York: Oxford University Press, 1995.

Erlewhine, Michael, ed. *All Music Guide to Country*. San Francisco:
Backbeat Books, 1997.

Escott, Colin. *The Grand Ole Opry: The Making of an American Icon*.
New York: Center Street Press, 2009.

Escott, Colin. *Lost Highway: The True Story of Country Music*.
Washington, DC: Smithsonian Books, 2003.

Escott, Colin. *Tattooed on Their Tongues: Lives in Country Music and
Early Rock and Roll*. New York: Schirmer Books, 1995.

Escott, Colin, George Merritt, and William MacEwen. *Hank Williams:
The Biography*. 2nd ed. Boston: Back Bay Books, 2009.

Ewing, Tom. *Bill Monroe: The Life and Music of the Blue Grass Man*.
Urbana: University of Illinois Press, 2018.

Feiler, Bruce S. *Dreamin' Out Loud: Garth Brooks, Wynonna Judd,
Wade Hayes, and the Changing Face of Nashville*. New York: Spike,
1999.

Gleason, Holly. *Woman Walk the Line: How the Women in Country
Music Changed Our Lives*. Austin: University of Texas Press, 2017.

Guralnick, Peter. *Lost Highway: Journeys and Arrivals of American
Musicians*. Boston: David R. Godine, 1979.

Horstman, Dorothy. *Sing Your Heart Out, Country Boy*. 3rd ed.
Nashville: CMF/Vanderbilt University Press, 1996.

Hubbs, Nadine. *Rednecks, Queers, and Country Music*. Berkeley:
University of California Press, 2014.

Hume, Margaret. *You're So Cold I'm Turning Blue: Guide to the
Greatest in Country Music*. New York: Penguin, 1982.

Jennings, Waylon, and Lenny Kaye. *Waylon: An Autobiography*.
New York: Grand Central Publishing, 2009.

Jensen, Joli. *Nashville Sound: Authenticity, Commercialization,
and Country Music*. Nashville: CMF/Vanderbilt University
Press, 1998.

Jones, George, with Tom Carter. *I Lived to Tell It All*. New York: Dell,
2014.

Kienzle, Rich. *Southwest Shuffle*. New York: Routledge, 2003.

Kingsbury, Paul, ed. *Country on Compact Disc: The Essential Guide to
the Music*. New York: Grove Press, 1993.

Kingsbury, Paul, ed. *The Country Reader: 25 Years of the* Journal of
Country Music. Nashville: Country Music Foundation Press, 1995.

Kingsbury, Paul, ed. *Will the Circle Be Unbroken: Country Music in
America*. New York: DK Publishing, 2006.

Lomax, John. *Adventures of a Ballad Hunter*. New York: Macmillan, 1947.

Lynn, Loretta, and George Vesey. *Coal Miner's Daughter*. Chicago: Contemporary Books, 1985.

Malone, Bill C. *Don't Get above Your Raisin': Country Music and the Southern Working Class*. Urbana: University of Illinois Press, 2001.

Malone, Bill C., and Tracey Laird. *Country Music U.S.A.* 50th anniversary ed. Austin: University of Texas Press, 2018.

Malone, Bill C., and Judith McCulloh, eds. *Stars of Country Music: Uncle Dave Macon to Johnny Rodriguez*. Urbana: University of Illinois Press, 1975.

McCall, Michael, and John Rumble, eds. *The Encyclopedia of Country Music*. New York: Oxford University Press, 2012.

McCloud, Barry. *Definitive Country: The Ultimate Encyclopedia of Country Music and Its Performers*. New York: A Perigree Book, 1995.

Nash, Alanna. *Behind Closed Doors: Talking with the Legends of Country Music*. New York: Knopf, 1988.

Neal, Jocelyn. *Country Music: A Cultural and Stylistic History*. 2nd ed. New York: Oxford University Press, 2019.

Nelson, Willie, and David Ritz. *It's a Long Story: My Life*. Boston: Little, Brown, 2015.

Peterson, Richard A. *Creating Country Music: Fabricating Authenticity*. Chicago: University of Chicago Press, 1999.

Porterfield, Nolan. *Jimmie Rodgers: The Life & Times of America's Blue Yodeler*. Urbana: University of Illinois Press, 1979.

Price, Robert E. *The Bakersfield Sound: How a Generation of Displaced Okies Revolutionized American Music*. Berkeley: Heyday, 2018.

Rosenberg, Neil V. *Bluegrass: A History*. Urbana: University of Illinois Press, 1985.

Russell, Tony. *Country Music Records: A Discography, 1921–1942*. New York: Oxford University Press, 2004.

Smith, Richard D. *Bluegrass: An Informal Guide*. Chicago: A Cappella Books, 1996.

Smith, Richard D. *Can't You Hear Me Callin': The Life of Bill Monroe, Father of Bluegrass*. New York: Little, Brown, 1999.

Stimeling, Travis D., ed. *Country Music Reader*. New York: Oxford University Press, 2015.

Stimeling, Travis D. *Oxford Handbook of Country Music*. New York: Oxford University Press, 2017.

Streissguth, Michael. *Outlaw: Waylon, Willie, Kris, and the Renegades of Nashville*. New York: Harper Collins/It Books, 2013.

Tichi, Cecelia. *High Lonesome: The American Culture of Country Music*. Chapel Hill: University of North Carolina Press, 1994.

Tosches, Nick. *Country: The Biggest Music in America*. 3rd ed. New York: Da Capo, 1996.

Tosches, Nick. *Where Dead Voices Gather*. New York: Little, Brown, 2001.

Townsend, Charles S. *San Antonio Rose: The Life and Music of Bob Wills*. Urbana: University of Illinois Press, 1976.

Wolfe, Charles K. *Classic Country*. New York: Routledge, 2000.

Wolfe, Charles K. *The Grand Ole Opry: The Early Years*. London: Old Time Music, 1978. Enlarged and revised as *A Good Natured Riot: The Birth of the Grand Ole Opry*. Nashville: CMF/Vanderbilt University Press, 1999.

Wolfe, Charles K. *Tennessee Strings: The Story of Country Music in Tennessee*. Knoxville: University of Tennessee Press, 1977.

Wolff, Kurt, and Orla Duane, eds. *Rough Guide to Country Music*. London: Rough Guides, 2000.

Zwanitzer, Mark. *Will You Miss Me When I'm Gone? The Carter Family and Their Legacy in American Music*. New York: Simon & Schuster, 2004.

Select Websites

Academy of Country Music: https://www.acmcountry.com/
American Banjo Museum: http://www.americanbanjomuseum.com/
Center for Popular Music: http://popmusic.mtsu.edu/
Center for Southern Folklore: https://www.southernfolklore.com/
Country Music Association: https://www.cmaworld.com/foundation/
Country Music Hall of Fame: https://countrymusichalloffame.org/
International Association for the Study of Popular Music (IASPM): http://www.iaspm.net/
International Bluegrass Music Association: https://ibma.org/
Society for Ethnomusicology: https://www.ethnomusicology.org/default.aspx
Southern Folklife Collection: https://library.unc.edu/wilson/sfc/

Index

A

"A Boy Named Sue," 91

"A Cowboy Has to Sing," 38

A Place in the Sun (album), 102

"A Poor Man's Roses," 105

"A Very Special Love Song," 72

"A White Sport Coat (and a Pink Carnation)," 63

Abbott (record label), 67, 71

AC/DC, 113

Ace in the Hole, 98

"Achy Breaky Heart," 115–116

"Act Naturally," 83, 95

Acuff, Roy, 40–42

Acuff-Rose (music publishers), 70

"Adios Amigo," 71

Adult contemporary music, 76

Aeroplane (album), 92

African American religious traditions, 12–13

African American spirituals, 12–13

African American traditional music, 12–14

"After All the Love Is Gone," 73

"After the Fire Is Gone," 73

"All Alone Am I," 70

All I Want (album), 102

"All My Ex's Live in Texas," 98

"All My Rowdy Friends (Have Settled Down)," 89

Alt-country, 111

American Ballads and Folk Songs (book), 11

American Idol (TV program), 116

American popular music, black and white influences on, 14

American Records (record label), 91

Americana music, 111

Anderson, Liz, 76

Anderson, Lynn, 76–77

Andrews Sisters, The, 53

Andy Griffith Show (TV show), 94

Anglin, Jack, 57

Anglo-American traditional music, 7–12

Anita Kerr Singers, 66–67, 71

"Another Lonely Song," 78

"Any Man of Mine," 113

"Apartment No. 9," 78

Appalachian Swing (album), 94

Archive of American Folk Song, Library of Congress, 11

"Are You from Dixie?," 43

Country Music

Armstrong, Louis, 33
Arnold, Eddy, 42, 70–71
"As Long as I Live," 57
Atkins, Chet, 65, 66–67, 87
"Austin," 115
Autry, Gene, 33, 35–37, 38, 41

B

"Back in the Saddle Again," 36
Bailey, DeFord, 29
Bakersfield Sound, 81, 82–85
"Ballad of John McEntire," 105
Ballads
  collectors of, 7–8
  defined, 7
  in the Appalachians, 8
Banjo
  classical or ragtime, 15–16
  clawhammer playing style, 15
  five-string, 14–16, 58
  West African predecessors of,
    14–15
Bate, Dr. Humphrey, 29
"Battle of New Orleans," 62
"Battle of the Alamo," 63
Beatles, The, 61, 73, 92, 95
Beaucoups of Blues (album), 95
"Bedtime Story," 78
"Behind Closed Doors," 72
Bennett, Tony, 55
Beverly Hillbillies, The (TV show),
    40
Beyoncé, 118
Big and Rich, 106
"Big Bang" of Country Music,
    6, 59
"Big Boss Man," 72
"Big Iron," 63
Blackstock, Narvel, 105
Blake, Norman, 92
"Blue," 114
"Blue Eyes Crying in the Rain,"
    87
Blue Grass Boys, 58

"Blue Moon of Kentucky," 59,
    60
Blue notes, 12
Blue Sky Boys, The, 35, 42–43
"Blue Suede Shoes," 61
"Blue Yodel" ("T for Texas"),
    5, 32
Bluebird Café, 106
Bluegrass music, 44, 49 50, 57–58
Blues, 13–14
Bolick brothers. *See* Blue Sky Boys,
    The
Bolick, Bill, 42
Bolick, Earl, 42
"Bouquet of Roses," 71
Boy bands, 109
Braddock, Bobby, 115
Bradley, Harold, 67
Bradley, Owen, 65, 67–68, 69, 74
"Branded Man," 85
Brazos Valley Boys, 56
"Break It to Me Gently," 70
Bristol, Tennessee, as location of
    the "big bang" of country
    music, 4, 5, 6, 19, 32
"Bro country," 118
Brockman, Polk, 21
Brooks, Colleen, 101
Brooks, Garth, 101–102, 103
Brother acts, 35, 42–44
Brown, Durwood, 45
Brown, Milton, 45
Brown, Zac, 109
Brumley, Tom, 82
"Buckaroo," 83
Buckaroos, The, 83
Buffalo Gun (movie), 63
"Bull and the Bear, The," 85
"Bully of the Town," 22
Bumgarner, Samantha, 23–24
Burns, Robert, 7–8
Burr, Gary, 103
"Bury Me beneath the Willow," 31
Bush, George W., 107
Byrds, The, 94, 95

C

Calloway, Cab, 45
Campbell, Glen, 92, 100
"Can't Even Get the Blues," 105
"Canned Head," 66
Capitol (record label), 49, 56, 61, 83, 85
Carey, Mariah, 118
Carnes, Kim, 80
Carpenters, The, 77
Carson, "Fiddlin'" John, 19, 20–21, 24
Carson, Kris. *See* Kristofferson, Kris
Carson, Rosa Lee, 22
Carter Family, The, 5–6, 30–31, 59, 66, 91
Carter, Alvin Pleasant (A. P.), 6, 30, 31
Carter, Mother Maybelle, 5, 31, 33, 67
Carter, Sara (Addington), 5–6, 31
Cash, Johnny, 81–82, 84, 86–87, 88, 90–92, 95
Cash, June Carter, 91
"Cattle Call," 71
Champion (horse), 36
Chandler, Dillard, 7
Chapin Carpenter, Mary, 97, 110–111
"Chatahoochee," 100
Child, Francis James, 7–8
Child ballads, 7–8
Christian, Charlie, 47
"Cigarettes, Whiskey, and Wild Women," 38
Ciminella, Christina. *See* Judd, Wynonna
"Cindy in the Summertime," 24
Clawhammer. *See* Banjo, clawhammer playing style
Clements, Vassar, 92
Cline, Patsy, 50, 68, 74, 86, 105, 114
"Coal Miner's Daughter," 74
"Coat of Many Colors," 75

Cohen, Paul, 57
"Cold, Cold Heart," 55
Cole, Nat "King," 67
Collins, Tommy, 82, 83
Colter, Jessi, 81, 85–86
Columbia (record label), 22, 23, 24, 77, 90, 110
Come on Over (album), 113
"Cool Water," 38
Cooley, Spade, 47
Coolidge, Rita, 88
Coon Creek Girls, 30
"Coon songs," 29
Cooper, James Fenimore, 10, 35
"Corn Licker Still in Georgia, A," 22–23
Country Gentleman (guitar), 66
"Country Gentleman," 66
Country radio, changes in the '80s and '90s to, 112
Country rock, 92–96
Countrypolitan music, 76–80
Cowboy Rides Again Tour, 98
Cowboy songs, 10–11
"Cowboy Take Me Away," 107
Cowboys, 10, 33, 35
Cowgirl singers, 38–40
Cramer, Floyd, 66, 67, 70, 71
"Crazy," 68, 86
Crosby, Bing, 41, 45
Crowell, Rodney, 96
Crudup, Blind Boy, 59
Curb (record label), 102
Cyrus, Billy Ray, 115–116

D

D (record label), 98
"Daddy Lessons," 118
Daily, Harold "Pappy," 79
Dalhart, Vernon, 25
Dance master, 8
Dance music, 8–9

"Dance, The," 101
Daniels, Charlie, 89
Davis, Eva, 23–24
Davis, Jimmie, 38
Deason, Muriel. *See* Wells, Kitty
Decca (record label), 11, 57, 67
"Delta Dawn," 114
Diamond Rio, 109
Dickens, Little Jimmy, 63
Dig Your Roots (album), 118
"Digging Up Bones," 99
Digital downloads of recordings, 112
Dillard, Doug, 93
Dillard, Rodney, 93
Dillards, The, 93–94
"Dim Lights, Thick Smoke (and Loud, Loud Music)," 52
Dion, Celine, 110, 113
"Dirt on My Boots," 117
"D-I-V-O-R-C-E," 78
Dixie Chicks, 107, 118
Dobro, 41, 92
"Does Fort Worth Ever Cross Your Mind?," 98
Dollywood (amusement park), 76
"Don't Be Stupid," 113
"Don't Come Home a-Drinkin' (with Lovin' on Your Mind)," 74
"Don't Fall in Love with a Dreamer," 80
"Don't It Make My Brown Eyes Blue," 77
"Don't Let Your Deal Go Down," 23
"Don't Rock the Jukebox," 100
"Don't Take the Girl," 102
"Door, The," 79
"Down at the Twist and Shout," 110
"Down, Down, Down," 49
Drifting Cowboys, The, 54
Driftwood, Jimmy, 62
Dulcimer, 17
"Dumb Blonde," 75

"Dum Dum," 70
Duncan, Tommy, 46–47
Dunn, Bob, 45
Dylan, Bob, 90, 92, 94, 95
"Dynamite," 69

E

Edwards, Eileen. *See* Twain, Shania
"Eighth of January," 62
"El Paso," 63
Electric guitar, 51–52
Epic (record label), 72, 77, 79
Estefan, Gloria, 113
Evans, Dale, 37
Everly Brothers, The, 95
"Every Time Two Fools Collide," 80
"Every Time You Touch Me," 72
Everywhere (album), 102
"Excuse Me, I Think I've Got a Heartache," 83

F

Faith (album), 103
Falsetto voice, 7, 22, 46
Fan Fair, 118
Fearless (album), 115
Female pioneers of country music, 23–25
Fiddle, 14, 16–18
Fiddle, portable, 9
First Edition, The, 79–80
Fisk University Singers, 13
Five-note (pentatonic) scale, 9
Flatt and Scruggs, 58
Flatt, Lester, 58
Florida Georgia Line, 118
Flying Burrito Brothers, 95
Foley, Red, 57
Folk balladeers, 61–63
Folk Song U.S.A., 11
"Fooling Around," 83
"Folsom Prison Blues," 90

"Fool No. 1," 70
"Forever and For Always," 114
"Four Walls," 71
Frailing. *See* Banjo, clawhammer
    playing style
"Friends in Low Places," 101
"From This Moment," 113
"Frosty the Snow Man," 36
Fruit Jar Drinkers, 29
"Fujiyama Mama," 61

G

Gaines, Chris. *See* Brooks,
    Garth
"Galloping on the
    Guitar," 66
"Gambler, The," 80
Gayle, Crystal, 77
Gene Autry's Melody Ranch,
    (radio show), 36
"Gentle on My Mind," 92
Gibson, Orville, 17
Gill, Vince, 96, 100
Glaser, Tompall, 86
Globe (record label), 56
"Golden Ring," 78
Golden West Cowboys, 41, 70
"Gone, Gone, Gone," 61
"Goodbye Earl," 107
Grand Ole Opry (radio show),
    25–30, 35, 41, 42, 52, 58, 60,
    63, 67, 68, 70, 71, 72, 116
"Grand Tour, The," 79
"Grandpa (Tell Me 'bout the Good
    Old Days)," 109
Gray, Zane, 35–36
Grayson and Whitter, 25
Grayson, G. B., 25
"Great Speckled Bird, The," 41
Greene, Richard, 94
Grisman, David, 94
Guitar, 16
Gunfighter Ballads and Trail Songs
    (album), 63

"Gunpowder 'n' Lead," 107
Guthrie, Jack, 49
Guthrie, Woody, 49
Guy, Aubrey Sheppard, 54, 89

H

Haggard, Merle, 47, 76, 81, 83,
    84–85, 86
"Hank the Hired Hand."
    See Thompson, Hank
Hank Williams Jr. and Friends
    (album), 89
"Happy Trails," 37
Harkreader, Sid, 29
Harman, Buddy, 66
Harmony Girls, The, 57
Harris, Emmylou, 95–96, 111
Harrison, George, 61
Hartford, John, 92
Hatcher, Lib, 99
Hay, George Dewey, 26–28, 29
"He Stopped Loving Her Today," 79
"He Thinks He'll Keep Her," 111
"Heartbreak U.S.A.," 57
Hee Haw (television show), 83–84
"Hell on Heels," 107
"Hello Darlin'," 73
"Hello Walls," 86
Helm, Levon, 109
"Help Me Make It through the
    Night," 88
"Here You Come Again," 76
"Hey Good Lookin'," 55
Highwaymen, The, 88
Hill, Faith, 102–103
Hillman, Chris, 95
Holland, W. S. "Fluke," 60
Holly, Buddy, 87
"Home on the Range," 11
Homer and Jethro, 66
"Honey Bop," 61
"Honey Don't," 61
Honky Tonk Heroes (album), 88
"Honky Tonk Man," 62

Honky-tonk music, 51–57
"Honky Tonkin'," 54
Horton, Johnny, 53, 62
"Hot Dog! That Made Him Mad," 61
Houston, Whitney, 75
"How Do," 110
Hubbard, Tyler, 118
"Hungry Hash House," 23
Hunks in hats, 99
"Hurt," 92
"Hushpuckena," 26

I

"I Can't Stop Loving You," 57
"I Cried (The Blue Right out of My Eyes)," 77
"I Did," 104
"I Don't Want to Play House," 78
"I Fall to Pieces," 68
"I Feel Lucky," 111
"I Guess I'm Crazy," 72
"I Hope You Dance," 107
"I Like It, I Love It," 102
("I Never Promised You a) Rose Garden," 76
"I Saw the Light," 54
"I Walk the Line," 90
"I Wanna Be a Cowboy's Sweetheart," 38
"I Wanna Play House with You," 71
"I Will Always Love You," 75
"I'll Go on Alone," 63
"I'll Wake You Up When I Get Home," 72
"I'm a Honky Tonk Girl," 74
"I'm a Lonesome Fugitive," 85
"I'm Getting Better," 71
"I'm Gonna Getcha," 114
"I'm Sorry," 70
"I'm That Kind of Girl," 104
"I've Got a Tiger by the Tail," 83
"Ida Red," 46
"If I Lose (Let Me Lose)," 23
"If My Heart Had Wings," 103

"If Tomorrow Never Comes," 101
"(If You're Not in It for Love) I'm Out of Here," 113
In Old Santa Fe (movie), 36
"In the Jailhouse Now," 33
"Indian Outlaw," 102
"Is This Me?," 71
"It Wasn't God That Made Honky Tonk Angels," 56, 57
"It's Alright to Be a Redneck," 100
"It's Only Make Believe," 73
"It's Your Love," 102

J

Jackson, Alan, 97–100
Jackson, Aunt Molly, 10–12
Jackson, Wanda, 61
"Jambalaya," 55
"Jay Gould's Daughter," 23
Jenkins, Harold. *See* Twitty, Conway
Jennings, John, 110
Jennings, Waylon, 81, 86, 87–88, 89
"John Hardy," 24
"Johnny Reb," 62
"Jolene," 75
Jones, George, 50, 77, 78–79
Jones, Grandpa, 29
Joplin, Janis, 88
Jordanaires, 66
Judd, Naomi, 108–109
Judd, Wynonna, 108–109
Judds, The, 107–109
"Just Between the Two of Us," 84
"Just Dropped In (to See What Condition My Condition Was In)," 80

K

Karpeles, Maude, 8
"Kaw-Liga," 56
"Keep on the Sunny Side," 30
Keillor, Garrison, 42

Kelley, Brian, 118
Kelley, Charles, 110
Kentucky Colonels, 94
Kerosene (album), 107
King, Carole, 110
King, Pee Wee, 41, 42, 70
Kingston Trio, The, 62
Kittredge, George Lyman, 10
KMBC (radio station), 40
"Knee Deep in the Blues," 63
Knight, Gladys, 88
Knocking. *See* Banjo, clawhammer
     playing style
KPHO (radio station), 63
Krauss, Alison, 111
Kristofferson, Kris, 2, 81, 86, 87, 88
KWKH (radio station), 52–53

L

L'Amour, Louis, 35
Ladies Love Outlaws (album), 87
"Lady," 80
Lady Antebellum, 109
Lair, John, 30
Lambert, Miranda, 106–107, 115
Lange, Robert "Mutt," 113, 114
"Last Roundup, The," 36
"Last Thing on My Mind," 75
Laugh-In (TV show), 83
Lawrence Welk Show, The (TV
     show), 76
"Leavin' on Your Mind," 68
Ledford, Lily May, 30
Ledford, Minnie, 30
Ledford, Rosie, 30
Lee, Brenda, 68, 69–70
"Let's Make Love," 103
Levon, 109
Lewis, Jerry Lee, 90
Light Crust Doughboys, The,
     44–45
Little Big Town, 109
"Little Miss Dyn-a-mite." *See* Lee,
     Brenda

"Little Old Log Cabin in the Lane,"
     21, 22
"Live Like You Were Dying,"
     103
"Liza Jane," 46
Lomax, Alan, 11–12
Lomax, John Avery, 10–11
"Lonely Again," 71
"Lonely Blue Boy," 73
"Lonely Too Long," 104
"Lonely Weekends," 72
"Lonesome Fugitive," 76, 85
"Losing You," 70
Louisiana Hayride, The (radio
     program), 49, 52–53, 54, 57,
     59, 67, 71
"Louisiana Woman, Mississippi
     Man," 73
"Love Can Build a Bridge,"
     109
Lovelace, Terry, 97, 104
Loveless, Patty, 96, 104–105
"Lovesick Blues," 55
"Lucille," 80
"Lucy Long," 15
Lunsford, Bascom Lamar, 24
Lynn, Loretta, 73, 74–75,
     77, 104
Lynn, Oliver "Mooney," 74, 75

M

Mabie, Milt, 40
Macon, "Uncle Dave," 28–29, 42
Maddox Brothers and Rose, The,
     48–49
Maddox, Rose, 48–49, 83
Maguire, Martie Erwin, 107
Maines, Natalie, 107
"Make Him a Soldier," 51
"Make the World Go Away," 71
"Mama He's Crazy," 109
"Mama Tried," 85
"Man! I Feel Like a Woman," 113
Mandolin, 16

Martin, Christian Friedrich (C. F.), 16
Massey, Curt, 40
Massey, Louise, 39–40
Maynard, Ken, 36
McAuliffe, Leon, 46, 47
McCarthy, Senator Joe, 62
McEntire, Pake, 105
McEntire, Reba, 105
McGee brothers, 29
McGraw, Tim, 102–103
McGraw, Tug, 102
McMichen, Clayton, 22
"Me and Bobby McGee," 88
"Mental Cruelty," 49
Mercury (record label), 113
"Mexican Joe," 71
MGM (record label), 46, 54, 89
Midland, 109
Midnight Jamboree (radio show), 54
Mills Brothers, The, 47
Minstrel music, 14–15, 29
Mitchell, Joni, 110
"Mohair Sam," 72
"Mommy for a Day," 57
Monroe Brothers, 43–44
Monroe, Ashley, 107
Monroe, Bill, 41, 42, 43–44, 49, 50, 57–58, 59, 68
Monroe, Birch, 43
Monroe, Charlie, 43
Montana, Patsy, 35, 38
"Moonshine Kate." *See* Carson, Rosa Lee
Morris, Maren, 118
"Most Beautiful Girl in the World, The," 72
"Move It on Over," 54
Muleskinner, 94
Murphy, Joaquin, 47
"Music Row," 67
Musical Brownies, The, 45
Muzik Mafia, 106
"My Adobe Hacienda," 40

"My Church," 118
"My Friends Are Gonna Be Strangers," 76, 85
"My Man (Understands)," 78

N

Nashville Skyline (album), 90, 95
Nashville Star (TV program), 116
National Barn Dance, The (radio show), 26, 30, 35, 38, 39, 41
NBC (radio network), 40–41
NBC Symphony Orchestra, 28
"Near You," 78
"Need You Now," 110
Nelson, Rick, 94
Nelson, Willie, 68, 81, 85, 86–87, 88, 89, 118
Newgrass Revival, 92
*Newly Discovered Early American Folk Song*s (album), 62
"9 to 5," 76
Nine Inch Nails, 92
"Nine Pound Hammer (Roll on Buddy)," 44
No Fences (album), 101
"Nobody's Darlin' But Mine," 38
Nolan, Bob, 37
Norris, Fate, 22
North Carolina Ramblers, 23
"North to Alaska," 62
Not a Moment Too Soon (album), 102

O

O Brother, Where Art Thou? (movie), 111
O'Daniel, W. Lee "Pappy," 45
OKeh (record label), 4, 18, 19, 21, 22, 24, 25
"Okie from Muskogee," 85
"Oklahoma's Yodeling Cowboy." *See* Autry, Gene

"Old Fashioned Washing Machine," 92
"Old Hen Cackled and the Rooster's Going to Crow," 21
"Old Shep," 7
"On the Other Hand," 99
"One by One," 57
Ossman, Vess L., 16
Oswald, "Bashful" Brother, 41
Our Singing Country (book), 11
Outlaw country, 81, 85–89
Owen, Fuzzy, 84
Owens, Bonnie Campbell, 83, 84, 85
Owens, Buck, 49, 61, 81, 82–84, 85, 95
Ozark Mountain Jamboree (radio program), 101

P

Paisley, Brad, 100
"Pan American Blues," 29
Pardi, John, 117
Parsons, Gram, 95, 96
Parton, Dolly, 74, 75–76, 96, 118
"Passionate Kisses," 111
Paxton, Tom, 75
Pearl, Minnie, 42
Peer, Ralph, 4–6, 19, 21, 31–32, 59
Perkins, Carl, 60–61, 90, 91
Perkins, Clayton, 60
Perkins, Luther, 90
Perry, Audrey Faith. *See* Hill, Faith
Petticoat Junction (TV show), 40
Phases and Stages (album), 86–87
"Philadelphia Lawyer," 49
Phillips, Sam, 58–59, 60–61
Pierce, Webb, 52–53
"Pill, The," 74–75
Pioneer Trio, The, 37

Pistol Annies, The, 107
Platinum (album), 106–107
Platinum High (movie), 73
Playford, John, 8
"Please Remember Me," 103
Poole, Charlie, 23
Prairie Home Companion, A (radio show), 42
Prairie Ramblers, The, 38
Presley, Angaleena, 107
Presley, Elvis, 33, 51, 59, 60, 62, 66, 67, 73, 90
Price, Ray, 86, 98
Progressive bluegrass, 92–96
Puckett, Riley, 22, 23–24, 31
Pugh, Virginia Wynette. *See* Wynette, Tammy
Pure Prairie League, 100
Puritan church, 9

R

"Race Is On, The," 79
Radio, early country music programs on, 25–30
"Rag Mop," 47
Rainwater, Cedric, 58
Raitt, Bonnie, 109
"Ramblin' Blues," 23
Ramey, Patty. *See* Loveless, Patty
Ramey, Roger, 104
Randolph, Boots, 66
Rapping. *See* Banjo, clawhammer playing style
Rascal Flatts, 109
Ray, Randy. *See* Travis, Randy
RCA Victor (record label), 4–6, 18, 31, 32, 33, 57, 59, 62, 66, 67, 71, 75, 86, 87, 92, 108
Record sales, ways of accounting for, 112
Recording industry, development of, 18
Red Headed Stranger (album), 87
Reeves, Jim, 53, 67, 71–72

Country Music

Religious songs, 9
Renfro Valley Barn Dance, The (radio show), 30
Republic Pictures, 42
Retro-country, 98–100
Reynolds, Allen, 77, 101
Rich, Charlie, 72
Rich, Don, 82
Richie, Lionel, 80
Riddle, Almeda, 7
Riddle, Leslie, 30–31
Rimes, LeAnn, 114
Ritter, Tex, 56
Robbins, Marty, 51, 62–63
Robertson, Eck, 18
Robinson, Martin David. *See* Robbins, Marty
Robison, Emily Erwin, 107
Robison, Fabor, 71
Rock 'n' Roll, rise of, 58–61
Rockabilly, 60–61
"Rockin' around the Christmas Tree," 69
"Rockin' with the Rhythm of the Rain," 109
Rodgers, Jimmie, 4–6, 31–33, 36, 46, 53, 59
Rogers, Kenny, 79–80, 99
Rogers, Roy, 33, 35, 37–38
Ronstadt, Linda, 96
"Roomful of Roses," 38
Rorer, Posey, 23
Rose, Fred, 41, 54, 87
Rowan, Peter, 94
Rubin, Rick, 91
"Ruby (Don't Take Your Love to Town)," 80
"Rudolf, the Red-Nosed Reindeer," 36
Russell, Leon, 87

S

"San Antonio Rose," 46
Sawyer Brown Band, 109

Scarecrow (album), 102
Scott, Sir Walter, 8
Scruggs, Earl, 58
Scruggs, Randy, 92
"Second Fiddle," 83
Sentimental ("heart") songs, 23
Sex Kittens Go to College (movie), 73
Shafer, Whitey, 98
"Shame, Shame on You," 47
Shape-note singing, 9, 31
Sharp, Cecil, 8
Shaver, Billy Joe, 88
"She Thinks I Still Care," 79
"She Was Only Seventeen," 63
"She's Not Just a Pretty Face," 114
Shelton, Blake, 115
Sherrill, Billy, 72, 77, 78–79
"Short Life of Trouble," 43
Shotgun Willie (album), 86
"Silver Haired Daddy of Mine, That," 36
Silverstein, Shel, 91
Simpson, Sturgill, 117
"Sing a Little Song of Heartache," 49
"Sing Me a Sad Song," 84
"Sing Me Back Home," 85
Singing masters, 9
"Singing My Song," 78
"Singing the Blues," 63
"Sink the Bismarck," 62
"Six More Miles (to the Graveyard)," 54
Skaggs, Ricky, 96, 100
"Skip to My Lou," 5
Slavery, 12
"Sleep, Baby, Sleep," 5
Slip-note (piano style), 67, 70
Slye, Leonard. *See* Rogers, Roy
Smith, Sammi, 88
"Smokin' and Drinkin'," 107
"Soldier's Joy," 22
"Solemn Old Judge, The." *See* Hay, George Dewey

"Something Like That," 103
Songster, 13
Sons of the Pioneers, 37, 38, 42
Speak Now (album), 115
Spencer, Tim, 37, 38
Stafford, Jo, 55
"Stairway of Love," 63
"Stand by Your Man," 78
"Standing in the Shadow (of a Very Famous Man)," 89
Stanley Brothers, 58
Stanley, Roba, 24, 25
Stapleton, Chris, 117
Starr, Ringo, 95
Steagall, Red, 105
Steel guitar, 41, 44, 46, 47, 52, 54
"Steel Guitar Rag," 46
Sterling records, 54
Stewart, Wynn, 84
Stone Canyon Band, 95
Stone, Harry, 41
Stoneman, Ernest, 4
"Storms Are on the Ocean, The," 30–31
Storms of Life (album), 99
"Story of My Life, The," 63
Strait Country (album), 98
Strait, George, 96, 97, 98
Stricklin, Al, 46
Stringbean, 29
"Such a Getting' Upstairs," 15
Sun (record label), 59, 60, 72, 77
"Sunday Morning Coming Down," 87, 88
"Sunny Side of Life," 43
Sutton, R. Glenn, 76
Sweeney, Joel Walker, 15
"Sweet Dreams," 68, 105
"Sweet Kitty Wells," 57
"Sweetest Gift (A Mother's Smile), The," 43, 51
Sweetheart of the Rodeo (album), 93, 94
Swift, Taylor, 97, 114–115

T

Take Me As I Am (album), 103
"Tall Dark Stranger," 83
Tanner, "Gid" (James Gideon), 22, 24
Tarpley, Brenda Mae. *See* Lee, Brenda
Taylor, Tut, 92
Teneva Ramblers, The, 5, 32
Tennessee Hillbillies, 57
Tennessee Mountain Boys, 57
"Tennessee Ploughboy, The." *See* Arnold, Eddy
Tennessee Two, The, 90
Texas Playboys, The, 45, 46, 47
Texas Troubadours, 53
"That Don't Impress Me Much," 113
"That's a No-No," 76
"That's Alright Mama," 59
"The Soldier's Sweetheart," 5
"This Kiss," 103
Thompson, Hank, 56, 61, 98
Thompson, Uncle Jimmy, 26
"Thumper Jones." *See* Jones, George
"Thunder Rolls, The," 101
"Tight Fittin' Jeans," 73
Tight-throated vocal style, 7
"Tim McGraw," 115
"Timber I'm Falling in Love," 104
"Tom Dooley," 62
"Top of the World," 77
Town Hall Party (TV show), 82
Travis, Merle, 56, 99
Travis, Randy, 96, 97, 98–99
Traywick, Randy Bruce. *See* Travis, Randy
Trigger (horse), 37
Trio (album), 96
Tubb, Ernest, 49, 50, 53–54, 68
Tucker, Tanya, 114
"Tumblin' Tumbleweeds" (song), 36, 38

Index

Tumbling Tumbleweeds (movie), 37
"Turn the World Around," 71
Twain, Shania, 97, 112–114
Twitty Birds, The, 73
Twitty City (amusement park), 73
Twitty, Conway, 72, 73, 77

U

"Under Your Spell Again," 83
"Unwound," 98
Up (album), 113–114
Upson, Dean, 52
Urban, Keith, 100

V

Vagabonds, The, 41, 42
Van Epps, Fred, 16
Vaqueros, 10
"Vice," 106–107
Victor (record label). *See* RCA Victor (record label)
Virginia Reelers, 22
Voice, The (TV program), 116

W

"Wabash Cannonball," 41
Wagoner, Porter, 75
"Waitin in Your Welfare Line," 83
"Waiting for a Train," 33
"Walking the Floor over You," 53
Wanted: The Outlaws (album), 86
Warner Brothers (record label), 89, 99
"Way You Love Me, The," 103
"Ways to Love a Man, The" 78
"We're Gonna Hold On," 78
Weavers, The, 61
Webb, Brenda Gail. *See* Gayle, Crystal
Webb, Loretta. *See* Lynn, Loretta
Weight of These Wings, The (album), 107

Weiss, Johnny, 47
Welch, Gillian, 111
"Welcome to My World," 71
Wells, Kitty, 49, 50, 56–57, 61, 74
West, Dottie, 80
Western Caravan (radio show), 63
Western swing, 44–49
Westerners, The, 39
"What Would You Give (in Exchange for Your Soul)," 43–44
"When It's Springtime in Alaska," 62
"When the White Azaleas Start Blooming," 40
"Where Were You (When the World Stopped Turning)," 100
White Stripes, 75
White, Clarence, 94
White, Jack, 75
White, Roland, 94
Whitman, Slim, 52
Whitter, Henry, 24–25, 62
"Whose Bed Have Your Boots Been Under," 113
"Wide Open Spaces," 107
"Wild One," 103
"Wild Side of Life, The," 56, 57
"Wildwood Flower," 31
"Will the Circle Be Unbroken," 31
Willburn Brothers, 104
Williams, Aubrey. *See* Guy, Aubrey Sheppard
Williams, Hank, 33, 49, 50, 52–53, 54–56, 62, 79
Williams, King Hiram. *See* Williams, Hank
Williams, Leona, 85
Williams, Lucinda, 111
Williams, Tex, 47
Williams, Jr., Hank 54, 88–89
Willie and Waylon (album), 88
Wills, Bob, 35, 45–47, 82, 98

Wills, Johnnie Lee, 47
Wilson, Gretchen, 106
Wise, Chubby, 58
WLS (radio station), 26, 38
Wolfe, Charles, 24
Womack, Lee Ann, 107
Woodlieff, Norman, 23
Work songs, 12
"Would You Lay with Me (in a Field
    of Stone)," 114
"Wreck of the Old 97," 25
"Wreck on the Highway," 41
Wright, Johnnie, 57
Wright, Louise, 57
"Wrong Road Again," 77
WSB (radio station), 21, 22,
    24, 26
WSM (radio station), 26–28,
    53–54
WSM Artists Bureau, 28
WSM Barn Dance (radio show),
    26
Wynette, Tammy, 65, 77–78, 79

Y

Yoakam, Dwight, 84
Yodeling, 33
"Yonder Comes a Sucker," 71
"You Ain't Woman Enough (to Take
    My Man," 74
"You and Me," 78
"You Are My Sunshine," 38
"You Can Feel Bad," 104
"You Never Miss Your Mother
    until She's Gone," 21
"You're Still the One," 113
"You're the Reason Our Kids Are
    Ugly," 73
Young, Faron, 86, 98
"Your Cheatin' Heart," 56
"Your Good Girl's Gonna Go
    Bad," 78

Z

Zero (record label), 74